Sleep
Sense

Sleep

Simple steps to a
full night's sleep
for babies and toddlers

Sense

Megan Faure & Ann Richardson

METZ PRESS

DEDICATION

This book is dedicated to Liz, Sheila, and Nazo. You have each
in the most special way shaped the mother in me. MF
I dedicate this book to Isabel Nkomo. AR

Published by Metz Press
1 Cameronians Avenue
Welgemoed, 7530 South Africa

First published in 2007
Reprinted 2008, 2009, 2010
Copyright © Metz Press 2007
Text copyright © Megan Faure, Ann Richardson
Illustrations copyright © Metz Press

Publisher & editor	Wilsia Metz
Design & lay-out	Paula Wood
Cover design	Paula Wood & Liezl Maree
Illustrations	Nikki Miles
Photograph Megan Faure	Ian Berril
Printing and binding	Creda Communications
ISBN	978-1-919992-79-2

Authors' acknowledgements

The way we see the world, the way we respond and the emotions we attach to events are predetermined by who and what we have interacted with previously. This book on sleep began eight years ago when my own first born taught me how tough sleep deprivation is. It is with immense empathy for sleep-deprived moms that I embarked on writing Sleep sense. My colleague Ann became part of the picture then, supremely wise in her advice on the practical management of sleep problems. Annie it is a privilege to share my book space with you again.

Over the past nine years, people such as Georgia DeGangi, Winnie Dunn, Astrid Berg, Bea Wirz, Mark Tomlinson and many of the professionals at the Infant Mental Health group I belong to, shaped the way I saw babies and their interactions with their mothers. It is because I really believe sleep is a mother-infant construct that I dedicate this book to the wonderful mothers in my life.

As with parenting and especially dealing with sleep problems, writing a book cannot be done without great support systems. With this in mind my greatest thanks goes to the love of my life Philip and to my God, who are my earthly strength and my hope. *Megan Faure*

Many folk helped to bring this book to fruition and to all these wonderful people, I thank you for your professional wisdom, your friendship, and your love and support. My husband Ken, and children Ellen and Maeve, were my constant rock and strength during this project – thank you for always being there for me. Special thanks to Sandy Hurwurth for her unfailing love and support. As always, unfailing gratitude to my Heavenly Father without whom nothing on earth would be possible. *Ann Richardson*

Combined thanks:
Wilsia, from Metz Press, thank you for believing in us once again and to Paula, too, who designed the book and works tirelessly on the Baby Sense vision. To our professional colleagues, Jayne Eurelle, Katherine Megaw, Diane Roslee, Dr Simon Strachan, Kerry Wallace, Dr Ashley Wewege, gratitude, as always, for your valuable and insightful input.

The scenarios and stories illustrated in this book are all true, taken either from babies seen in practice, from Internet questions or from our children. All names have been changed to protect the precious confidence we respect. Thanks goes to these mothers and babies who daily remind us how devastating sleep deprivation is and have taught us not to overlook the simplest reason when dealing with sleep problems.

And last but not least, all thanks to our super star 'second moms' of our homes, Isabel Nkomo and Nazo Mtambeki who keep the home fires burning for us whilst we do what we do – God bless you both.

Foreword

In the early months of life, the baby learns to regulate sleep-wake cycles. Caregivers help support the baby by establishing set times for naps and bedtime and enacting bedtime rituals. The baby learns how to self-calm by using soothing devices in the crib. This helps the child to fall asleep on his own. The young infant also learns to tolerate a range of sensory experiences and to balance states of arousal and alertness. Parents help their baby by avoiding over stimulation. As young babies develop and grow, the parent plays an important role by providing experiences that support attachment and separateness.

As the child develops into the second and third years of life, sleep takes on new meanings. The child learns to self-calm after a stimulating day of activities. Parents help by providing their child with a balance between sensory stimulation and calming activities. Negotiating fears of dark places and of being alone emerge for the toddler. And before long, the young child asserts his autonomy while learning to tolerate limits set by their caregivers around bedtime rituals.

For many children, these stages of sleep do not go smoothly. There are many reasons that things become difficult. The child may struggle with the task of falling and staying asleep because they have not learned to self-regulate sleep-wake cycles. Some children do not know how to self-soothe or they become easily over-stimulated by sensory experiences. An anxiously attached baby will cling to their parent and be fearful to be alone for sleep. A wilful toddler may assert: "No! I'm not going to bed!" Whatever the reasons, parents need a good resource to figure out what might be causing their child to have difficulties in falling and staying asleep at night.

Sleep sense is just the book to help parents with this difficult task. It is a beautifully written, comprehensive resource book on sleep management for infants, toddlers, and preschoolers. The authors convey with warm sensitivity the struggles that parents experience. Like the child, the parents quickly become sleep deprived just by parenting a sleepless child. The authors help parents to understand what may underlie the sleep problem by providing developmental information and relevant case examples to depict the common types of sleep problems. A unique aspect of this book is the discussion of how sensory problems may contribute to the sleep disturbance.

Sleep sense is well grounded in developmental research and should be very helpful to parents in understanding the relationship between sleep patterns and typical development. The authors' philosophy is one that integrates the importance of balancing sensory stimulation experienced in everyday life with regular routines of self-soothing. Ms. Faure and Ms. Richardson emphasize the importance of learning to respond in sensitive, caring, and appropriate ways to the infant's signals, thus strengthening the attachment bond between parent and child. The book provides advice on how to establish a reasonable and well-balanced schedule of daily activities to foster sleep while making modifications in the sleep environment to promote better sleep. The philosophy underlying the suggestions in the book is that infants and young children need to become proficient self-soothers and, to become emotionally healthy, they need to develop warm and secure attachments with their caregivers in order to separate for sleeping alone.

This book is full of practical advice on breaking unhealthy sleep habits while addressing common problems such as heightened arousal, sensory hypersensitivities, nightmares and fears, and separation anxiety that may disrupt sleep. Strategies are presented on how to break co-sleeping when the child is developmentally ready to sleep alone. The format of the book is accessible and easy to read for the tired parent. This is a must-have book for parents of young babies and toddlers. It is also an excellent resource book for professionals working in early intervention.

GEORGIA DEGANGI, PH.D.

(Dr. DeGangi is a clinical psychologist and occupational therapist and is well-known for her work with infants and children with regulatory disorders. She has a clinical practice at ITS for Children and Families, Inc. in Kensington, MD. USA and is co-chair of the infant/young child mental health program at the Washington School of Psychiatry.)

Contents

Section 2

Introduction

Why *Sleep sense* is a different approach to sleep, one that works well for you and gently for your baby.

If you are reading this book you are no doubt experiencing problems with your baby's sleep. You may have read countless books, tried a myriad of suggestions, but still find yourself suffering from lack of sleep. Other parents, family members and even professionals may have labelled your baby's sleep behaviour as anything from 'normal' to 'naughty'. You have probably been advised by now to just accept the lack of sleep or you may have been told to close the door and just 'let your baby cry it out'.

If you have tried various forms of controlled crying unsuccessfully, you may be feeling pretty desperate. Unless sleep training is done with an understanding of all of your baby's needs, it is unlikely to be successful, which is why you may well have thrown in the towel by now, giving up in desperation and be saying that 'nothing works'.

SO WHAT DO YOU NEED TO DO TO GET A GOOD NIGHT'S SLEEP?

There is a process for establishing good sleep patterns. This process is simple to implement and so 'sensible' that you will wonder why you have not thought of it before.

The start of the process is to **understand how your baby sleeps** so that you will have realistic expectations about when to expect a full night's sleep. Babies and toddlers can and should be able to sleep independently. This independence develops as babies get older and most babies need some assistance to get it right.

You then go on to lay the foundation for good, healthy sleep habits, by **setting the stage** for good sleep. In the first half of this book there are nine easy steps that you need to follow from the word go, if possible, to prime your baby for good and restful sleep. If your baby is under four months of age you will find that by implementing these strategies you will have no need to ever contemplate sleep training.

If you have not followed these steps, this may well be the reason why you are still having sleep problems, and why sleep training has not worked for you yet. These nine steps need to be in place before you can confidently embark on a sleep-training programme.

Once you have set the stage for sleep, the next step, is to **teach your baby** to put himself to sleep, not only at bedtime, but in the middle of the night as well, should he wake for no physical reason. The ***Sleep sense*** approach to sleep coaching is gentle and based on the natural and age-appropriate capacity your baby has for self calming or soothing, and for separation from you.

Teaching your baby to sleep, if done at an appropriate age, is something that can be achieved without too much difficulty.

Understanding sleep, setting the stage and sleep coaching are handled in the first part of the book.

In the second part of *Sleep sense*, you will find quick and easy age-appropriate quick relief solutions for your baby's sleep problems. If you choose to jump straight to the quick relief sections (understandable when you are feeling desperate), it is recommended that you read the chapter related to your baby's specific sleep problem as well as the quick relief chapter for his age.

Sleep sense is not a general baby-care book and does not cover stimulation, development, feeding or health comprehensively. For this information refer to our earlier books, *Baby sense* or *Toddler sense*. *Sleep sense* does not override the advice of your paediatrician. If your baby is ill, was premature or is failing to thrive, you need to seek the advice of your doctor before dealing with sleep problems.

Setting the stage for sleep

Paving the way for good sleep habits from day one
to the toddler years

Set the stage

Have appropriate expectations for your baby's sleep

Ensure her daily sensory experiences prime her for a good night's sleep

Your baby's sleep environment must support sleep

Rule out hunger as the cause of night wakings

Eliminate any organic or medical reasons for sleeplessness

Establish healthy day sleeps for healthy night sleep

Prime your baby for independent night soothing with good sleep associations

Deal with separation issues as they arise

Teach your baby to re-settle himself

Sleep diary before Sleep sense

Before embarking on the **Sleep sense 9 steps**, we suggest you take the time to record your baby's sleep patterns for at least two consecutive nights. This will help you recognise areas for improvement, ensure your expectations are correct and highlight improvement after a week or two. The sleep diary is divided into blocks of 30 minutes, beginning at 6 am, through to 5:30 am.

Week date: _____   **Baby's age:** _____

1. Where do you you prepare your baby for sleep? In his sleep zone, the car or anywhere in the house? _____

2. Note relevant points about the sleep zone: lighting, cot, bedding etc. _____

Awake: Leave all blocks when your baby is awake blank; this will highlight how much time your baby spends awake between sleeps during the day.

Trying to settle or fighting sleep: Put a diagonal line through all blocks when you are trying to get your baby to sleep. In the space below these blocks record what interventions you are implementing to calm your baby or get him to sleep.

Asleep: Shade all blocks when your baby is asleep. Under each shaded block you can record where and how your baby sleeps, for example very restless, dead still, noisy etc.

DAY	6	7	8	9	10	11	12	1 pm	2	3	4	5	6	7	8	9	10	11	12	1 am	2	3	4	5
1																								
2																								
3																								
4																								
5																								
6																								

Sleep 101

CHAPTER 1

STEP 1: HAVE APPROPRIATE EXPECTATIONS FOR YOUR BABY'S SLEEP

It was the first time since university that Nicky, Daniela and Jenny had got together and now look at them - all grown up with babies! They had to admit that they would rather be dealing with final year exams than the sleepless nights they were now experiencing. Nicky had heard that she could reasonably expect her six week old to sleep through but he still woke three times at night. Daniela was becoming increasingly frustrated at her baby boy waking after 45 minutes at every day sleep – weren't babies supposed to sleep, well, like babies? Jenny was the most experienced mom, with a four-year-old and a two-year-old but she was desperately trying to make them sleep past 5 am by keeping her toddlers up later at night. Over dinner the three friends agreed that had 'Sleep 101' been offered at university it would have been the most useful course they could have done!

Sleep deprivation is known as being possibly one of the worst forms of torture, but until you are a parent you do not really understand this. Being woken from a deep sleep at night as your baby cries out has the potential to make any parent's blood curdle and their heart miss a beat. Knowing how important sleep is for our well being and how devastating the lack thereof, it's surprising how little is actually understood about sleep and how many fallacies abound about this precious commodity.

We believe that having a proper understanding of sleep is the first vital step to dealing with sleep problems. Please read this chapter carefully as it will aid you in sorting out your baby's sleep problems for two reasons:

- By having a good understanding of sleep, you will have **reasonable expectations** of your baby. You may realize that your baby's wakings and your broken sleep are temporary and related to your baby's age and you will thus react in a less negative way to sleep deprivation caused by broken sleep.
- If your baby is waking more than he should for his age, you will be empowered to implement strategies to change your baby's sleep habits for the better. By understanding how babies sleep, you will be able to remedy problem areas and **implement effective sleep coaching**.

THE IMPORTANCE OF SLEEP

"A person will die from total lack of sleep quicker than they would from starvation. Death will occur in about ten days without sleep, while starvation takes a few weeks."

The World's Most Amazing Science Facts

The fact that you are reading this book means that you probably don't need anyone to tell you that you need sleep. But it's not just in your mind. Research indicates that sleep-deprived parents face a significantly increased risk of involvement in road accidents, postnatal depression and decreased performance at work. Sleep is the power source that keeps your mind alert and calm. Lack of sleep wears down your immunity, sex drive, your thought processes and emotional resilience. And yet it's in a sleep-deprived state that we engage in the most important role of our lives: parenting.

Babies and toddlers are also very negatively affected by fatigue. They are less able to deal with **normal separations** from their moms or caregivers, and as toddlers have a higher propensity to throw **temper tantrums**. Their **social functioning** is marked by grumpy unpredictability and they are less able to self calm when confronted with frustrations such as toy sharing. In the long term, as well as not benefiting optimally from their world, sleep-deprived toddlers may have hampered ability to deal with **stress**. At the critical stage when toddlers are learning the skills needed to deal with stress, a sleep-deprived child is too fatigued to learn positive **coping mechanisms**, such as delayed gratification, to see him through later life.

For these reasons, you need to address your baby or toddler's sleep issues as a matter of urgency. Whether you are beginning the journey of changing your child's sleep patterns for the better, or adopting a pro-active approach to get it right from the word go to prevent sleep problems from arising at a later stage, this chapter will clarify the way babies and toddlers sleep and will thereby equip you with the necessary knowledge to tackle the task ahead confidently.

LENGTH OF DAY SLEEPS: WHAT TO EXPECT

Daniela was frustrated by Joshua waking after 45 minutes of sleep during the day; she expected to be able to have a shower, do the laundry and grab a cup of coffee all while her new baby slept. It came as a surprise that since the age of three weeks, he would not sleep for long stretches.

The reason that babies frequently wake after 45 minutes of sleep is that they are waking at the end of a sleep cycle. Knowing just how these cycles work, will ensure that you have reasonable expectations of your baby's sleep and help you find strategies to lengthen day sleeps by assisting your baby to link sleep cycles.

Sleep cycles

Your baby has three obvious stages of sleep: The first stage of sleep is the **drowsy state**, a state of sleepy wakefulness, in which your baby is preparing for sleep, cuddling down and experiences blurry-eyed blinks as his body shifts down a state.

The second major stage of sleep is called **light sleep**. In light sleep your baby experiences **REM** (Rapid Eye Movement) **sleep**, so called as his eyes are moving under the lids as he dreams. Adults spend a small portion of their sleep time in REM sleep – mainly in the early morning, and experience paralysis of the limbs during this stage. Your baby, on the other hand, is in REM sleep for almost half of his sleep time and experiences many body twitches and movements whilst dreaming. In this light sleep state, your baby will be easily woken by sounds and other sensory input in the environment. This is one of the reasons babies don't sleep as well as older children and adults who spend more time in the deep sleep state.

As your baby falls deeper into sleep, he experiences a small but sudden jerk of his muscles, called a **hypnagogic startle**. Adults, too, experience this jerk, but in babies it can be sufficient to wake them up.

Your baby then transitions into **non-REM sleep**. During this stage, your baby does not dream or move, and may be hard to wake. This deep-sleep state of sleep is vital for our health, as it is in this stage that most of the processes aimed at the maintenance and repair of our body take place. It is also the sleep stage in which growth hormone is secreted in the greatest quantities, which is essential for your baby's growth. This is but one of the reasons why it is important for your baby's health and development to have periods of deep sleep.

After 30 minutes of sleep, your baby will begin to move back into lighter sleep and finally back into a very light sleep state where he is very likely to wake. The process of becoming drowsy and falling asleep, moving into deep sleep and back into a light sleep state is called a **sleep cycle**. An adult sleep cycle lasts about 90 minutes, a toddler's sleep cycle is about an hour and a baby's 45 minutes.

> **SLEEP SECRET**
> If your baby wakes within 15 minutes of going down or is a 'cat napper', it may well be this little jerk that is waking him. This is particularly evident in newborns and is best managed by swaddling your baby tightly in a stretchy cotton blanket.

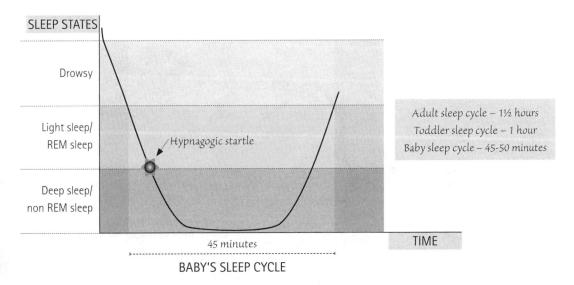

SLEEP STATES

Drowsy

Light sleep/ REM sleep

Hypnagogic startle

Deep sleep/ non REM sleep

Adult sleep cycle – 1½ hours
Toddler sleep cycle – 1 hour
Baby sleep cycle – 45-50 minutes

45 minutes

TIME

BABY'S SLEEP CYCLE

In the early days, your baby may sleep for very long stretches. He will then go through a period of waking from most sleeps after 45 minutes. By six months of age your baby should have learnt to link sleep cycles and transition back into deep sleep for at least one day sleep. At this stage, an aim of sleep coaching will be to assist your baby to link sleep cycles and to sleep for longer than 45 minutes at one day sleep and during the night.

SLEEP REJUVENATION: WHAT TO EXPECT

Jenny was tired of not feeling rejuvenated when she woke after a night of broken sleep. She also expected her toddlers to wake cheerful and refreshed no matter how long they had slept and yet they often woke very grumpy, especially after their afternoon naps. Why is it that sleep sometimes leaves us feeling more tired?

The effect of sleep on our mood and health has largely to do with its effect on the brain. Cycling in and out of sleep states has been understood for years but very recent literature reveals a new hypothesis of why each sleep state is vital for our health. Non-REM sleep in particular is so important that if your baby is woken during this deep sleep state or if he wakes frequently at night not allowing him adequate deep sleep time, he will feel fractious, irritable and not rejuvenated.

The effect of sleep

It is surprising to know that on the day of your baby's birth he had every brain cell he needs. In the early days when your baby's brain is developing at a rapid rate, vital connections are made between these brain cells (neurons). Neurons that are not connected or used are lost. It is literally a case of **use it or lose it**. Sleep impacts on the development of these neural connections and thus your baby's development.

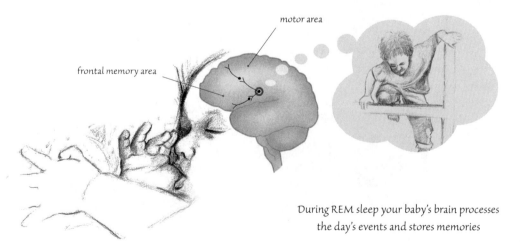

motor area

frontal memory area

During REM sleep your baby's brain processes the day's events and stores memories

- **REM sleep** is the sleep state in which we make vital connections (synapses) between brain cells as we process what we have experienced through our senses during the day. For instance, while your baby sleeps the sound of your voice is programmed into his brain with all the positive feelings he associates with you. And while your toddler dreams about climbing up the slide, his motor cortex in the brain hardwires the memory of climbing which he will put to good use the next time he plays on a slide. Infancy is the stage when your baby's brain is making connections and learning so much, which explains why your baby's sleep is made up of so much REM time compared to the time you spend in REM sleep.

SLEEP SECRET
During REM sleep the information derived from sensory input is processed in the brain, connections between brain cells are made, and the storage and memory of information take place.

- **Non-REM sleep**, on the other hand, is just as important for us all. Not for the forming of connections (or synapses), but for the opposite: breaking or pruning the connections! As strange as this sounds, pruning of the synapses in the brain is also a vital brain function to enable us to cope. By doing so, we process and memorize only the **essentials** of our daily experiences. Each day we process so much sensory information that our body would be unable to cope with the energy demands our brain would make if it just kept growing. We would also be susceptible to overload if our brain became an infinite web of synapses or connections. So because our body recognizes that our brain needs to 'slow down for repairs' we go into non-REM sleep. While the rest of the body is in a state of rest, the brain is hard at work pruning the branches or connections that are not useful. This is why good deep sleep states are vital for you and your baby.

NIGHT WAKINGS: WHAT TO EXPECT

Max and Jack may have been cousins but they were such different toddlers. Max gave his mom an easy time. Although she heard him waking at night and searching for his teddy, he hardly ever called her in. Jack, on the other hand, was giving his mom a really tough time. He was waking at least seven times at night, refusing to go back to sleep unless his mom stayed with him, and she was falling apart. Why is it that some babies are easy and others are not and what is reasonable to expect?

SLEEP SECRET
Sleep deprivation or broken sleep, preventing us from entering into a state of deep sleep, will inhibit this active process of restoration and repair, which will undoubtedly leave us feeling overloaded and fractious.

Between sleep cycles, when we are in the light sleep state, we regain semi-consciousness or may even wake partially at night before resettling. Before your pregnancy, you were probably unaware of these semi-conscious states or light wakings you experienced at night and woke in the morning feeling like you had a full night's sleep. Late in pregnancy your discomfort caused you to rouse fully between some sleep cycles to go to the toilet, or change position etc. Like adults, young babies come into a light sleep state (semi-consciousness) between sleep cycles, as frequently as every 45 minutes. All babies stir during this light sleep state, and some may even wake up. So why is it that babies like Max appear to sleep through and those like Jack wake during every light sleep state?

Good sleepers vs. poor sleepers

All babies and toddlers wake at least briefly one to three times each night after 4-6 hours of sleep. Between sleep cycles, **'good sleepers'** wake into a drowsy or light sleep state, turn over and resettle into the next sleep cycle independently – we call these babies **self-soothers** because they can self-soothe back to sleep. (See Chapter 7 for self-soothing strategies.)

'Poor sleepers' need intervention for whatever reason to resettle into the next sleep cycle. This may happen one to three times in a night or as often as every sleep cycle (every 45-50 minutes). We call these babies **signallers**.

For at least the first three months, when babies wake they call for attention owing to a real basic need, such as hunger. As babies mature and their basic needs for nutrition or comfort decrease, most of them gradually learn (as a result of to neurological maturation) to switch from **signalling to self-soothing**.

But the question is when should babies start to resettle themselves and self-soothe, or, as the common question goes: 'when should my baby sleep through?'

Keep reading to learn more about the secrets of healthy sleep habits and begin to look forward to some more precious sleep.

SLEEPING THROUGH: WHAT TO EXPECT

Like many moms, Nicky has heard that her baby should be able to sleep through the night by six weeks of age and that once her baby has achieved this, she will never look back.

This fallacy leaves little room for individual variances and leaves many parents feeling despondent. What is reasonable to expect?

The most frequently asked question: 'when should my baby sleep through?' is one that always needs answering. The answer is really determined by what is reasonable to expect from your baby:

• Firstly, it needs to be pointed out that sleeping through for a baby, **constitutes sleeping 8-10 or more hours at a stretch without waking up fully** and needing any intervention from a care giver in order to settle. Thus, if your baby's bedtime is between 6 pm and 7 pm (as it should be) you can expect a waking at between 3 am and 5 am, depending on your baby's age. Many babies will go back to sleep after this time with a feed (if age appropriate), a quick pat or a cuddle. If your toddler wakes for the day at this time, keep interactions muted (let him know this is not play time) and take him quietly into your bed and with a bit of luck he will fall back to sleep.

• Under six months of age, young babies have nutritional needs at night that gradually decrease as they get older. Having said this, some babies do sleep through the night before three months of age but many of these will experience a shift in sleep patterns once again owing to growth spurts. Most babies can be expected to sleep through the night from between **four to six months old**– in other words, manage to last without a feed for a period of about 8-10 hours.

- Like other developmental milestones, sleep has certain norms that are obviously as variable as any other milestone. The following are some guidelines for sleep stretches at night:

Age	Sleep at night	Hours sleep/24 hours
0-2 weeks	Little differentiation between day and night. Expect sleep to happen in between feeds, which will most likely be on demand,	Most of a 24 hour period except when feeding
2-6 weeks	One 4-5 hour stretch after one of the night feeds (usually in the first part of the evening) and anything between 2-4 hour stretches thereafter.	18-20 hours
6-12 weeks	One 6-7 hour stretch from bedtime to the first night feed and anything between 3-4 hour stretches thereafter.	16-18 hours
3-6 months	One 8-10 hour stretch from bedtime to the early hours of the morning, and then a 3-4 hour stretch thereafter.	14-18 hours
6-24 months	10-12 hour stretch from bedtime until the first early morning feed.	12-16 hours
3-5 years	11-12 hour stretch through the night. Day sleep usually falls away around this time.	12 hours

Points to consider

- If your baby is ill, it is unlikely he will sleep soundly; he may wake frequently for comfort. He may need to be offered fluids regularly if he is dehydrated. Remember to shift your expectations of sleep if this is the case.
- If your baby had a low birth weight, was born prematurely or is not thriving, he will most likely sleep through later than other babies.
- In healthy babies over six months of age, sleeping through is not just an unattainable luxury; it's a developmental necessity. You are not unreasonable in your expectation of a good night's sleep for your baby if he is well and thriving.

> SLEEP SECRET
> Keep in mind that your expectations of sleep may differ from what your baby is actually capable of, in terms of sleep ability.

- When beginning to solve your baby's sleep problems, the first step is to **understand the basics** of baby sleep so that your expectations are reasonable and your interventions meaningful.
- **Sleep is important** for your emotional, physical and mental health but also for your baby's growth, immunity and emotional development. There are endless reasons for you to sort out your baby's sleep problems and get a good night's sleep.
- A baby's **sleep cycle** is made up of a similar amount of light and deep sleep, both equally important. Light sleep is important for processing sensory information and making sense of the world around us. Deep sleep prevents over-stimulation through a process of pruning redundant brain connections.
- As your baby descends into deeper sleep or during the REM sleep state (light sleep) he may be disrupted by **small jerks** that are sufficient to wake him resulting in cat-napping. These disruptions prevent deep sleep, therefore your baby will be susceptible to over-stimulation and fussing.
- Ensure that your **expectations** of when your baby will sleep through are appropriate and if they are, deal with your baby's sleep problems by first setting the stage for sleep and, if necessary, sleep training your baby.

STEPS TO A GOOD NIGHT SLEEP

Many new concepts have been introduced in this chapter, some of which may appear a little theoretical. Be assured that this understanding of sleep forms the foundation upon which you will build the structure of healthy sleep. Read on for the other eight steps to a good night's sleep.

Sensory secrets for sleep

CHAPTER 2

STEP 2: ENSURE YOUR BABY'S DAILY SENSORY EXPERIENCES SUPPORT HEALTHY SLEEP

It was the first time Angi had left Tom for any length of time, but she felt that at 19 months he would cope fine and was in good hands with his granny. She had been looking forward to doing the Otter Trail for ages. Waking up on the second morning of the hike she could not remember when last she had slept so well. The beds were basic stretchers and her sleeping bag was not as soothing as her heavy feather duvet at home, but Angi realized that all the exercise of the hike, along with the sea air and the sound of the waves breaking on the shore was just what the doctor ordered for a sleep-deprived mom!

Angi's realization could well hold the key to helping her solve her toddler's sleep issues when she returns home. Our sensory environment such as the sensory experiences we have during the day, as well as what is happening in our sensory world just before bedtime, all have a huge effect on sleep. In both establishing good sleep habits for your baby and solving deeply-entrenched sleep problems in your toddler you need to make sure your child's daily sensory experiences are priming him for good sleep.

SENSORY ISSUES

Sensory issues may be contributing to sleep problems if your child
- Fights sleep as soon as he is put down for day or night sleeps
- Does not generally have day sleeps, and is inclined to rather 'cat nap' fitfully throughout the day.
- After fighting sleep at bedtime, tends to fall dead asleep and then repeatedly wakes every 45 minutes, never linking sleep cycles, especially in the early evening
- Is a restless, noisy sleeper who seems to need to move about his cot at night
- Is very stimulated by his caregivers and socialises a lot, resulting in a busy or fussy child
- Appears to crave stimulation, resulting in a busy, but sometimes fussy child, especially as the day progresses.
- Rocks or bangs his head vigorously when trying to fall asleep and/or wakes up head banging in the middle of the night

SLEEP SECRET
Being in tune to your
baby's sensory world
as you begin to set him
up for good sleep habits
(by setting the stage for
sleep), or as you tackle
deeply entrenched
sleep problems, lays the
foundation for healthy
sleep forever.

SENSORY LOAD AND STATE

Every waking and sleeping moment, our brains take in sensory information via our senses of hearing, smell, sight, taste and touch plus our hidden senses of body position (proprioception) and movement (vestibular system). Our internal organs also supply our brain with information – such as being hungry, or needing to pass a wind – this sense is called interoception.

Much of the time we are unaware of the sensory information our wonderfully complex brain is processing. But whether we are aware of the sensory input or not, it has an effect on our state and how we feel and behave.

Babies have six behavioural states: deep sleep, light sleep, drowsy state, calm alert, active alert and crying (Brazelton, 1984). The **type** of sensory information we receive determines to a large degree which state we are in.

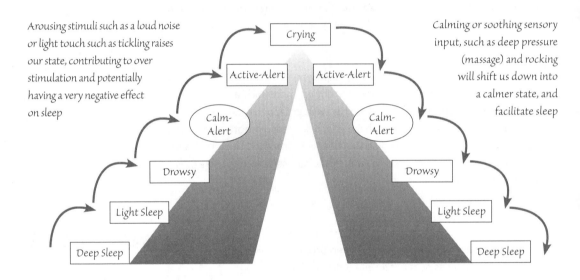

Arousing stimuli such as a loud noise or light touch such as tickling raises our state, contributing to over stimulation and potentially having a very negative effect on sleep

Calming or soothing sensory input, such as deep pressure (massage) and rocking will shift us down into a calmer state, and facilitate sleep

Crying

Active-Alert   Active-Alert

Calm-Alert   Calm-Alert

Drowsy   Drowsy

Light Sleep   Light Sleep

Deep Sleep   Deep Sleep

The effect of stimulation on sleep

If your baby is over stimulated or does not have the opportunity to calm down before sleep, he will battle to shift into a drowsy state and fall asleep independently. Understanding the role of calming sensory input is your first step towards inducing and enhancing sleep. Calming sensory input should be used very specifically **during the day, just before sleep, in the sleep zone and while your baby is asleep**.

STIMULATION DURING THE DAY

Think back to a time when you were exposed to highly stimulating input whilst attending a course, working on a deadline or learning a new skill. You may well have battled to fall asleep that evening and may even have woken in the night to process some new ideas. While it is cognitive stimulation that keeps us adults awake at night, it is *sensory stimulation* that affects your baby's sleep. A busy day, packed with new learning experiences and social situations can be very over-stimulating for your little one.

Stimulation is important but if your baby is battling to fall asleep at bedtime or waking frequently in the middle of the night, you could well be over-stimulating him during the day. So, how do we know when it is too much? Follow these simple guidelines to make sure your little one is not in a permanent state of over-stimulation.

Respond to your baby's signals

Limit stimulation in response to your baby's signals. While stimulation is important, it is essential to follow your baby's lead as to how much is enough. Warning signs of over-stimulation are easy to miss if you don't know what you are looking for, and they are easily misinterpreted as boredom, colic or naughtiness. (For full details on your baby's signals, refer to *Baby sense*, Megan Faure & Ann Richardson, 2002, Metz Press.) If your baby has been awake for a while, look for these signals that he has had enough:

- When your **young baby** starts looking away (and won't re-engage eye contact with you), sucks vigorously on his hands, loses interest in his feed, or arches his body away from you, he may be indicating that he has had enough stimulation. Signals such as sneezing, yawning or hiccupping may also be indications that your baby is becoming overloaded.
- Your **older baby** may start to search for his security object (dummy or sleep blanky), he may move away from a person or activity and begin to fidget and whine, indicating that he has had enough stimulation.
- Look out for the signals in your **toddler** that tell you he is getting over-stimulated, such as becoming clingy and irritable, refusing to eat or co-operate and biting or pushing other children.

This is the time to introduce some calming strategies, such as a walk with him snuggled up close to you in a pouch or sling or just playing some music with no activity or visual stimuli accompanying it. Use nature's calming environment, such as watching trees blow in the breeze to effectively calm your little one down.

SLEEP SECRET
Recent research has shown that time in sunlight during the day also enhances babies' sleep. Always apply appropriate sun block and put a hat on your baby's head when you expose him to the sun.

LIMIT YOUR BABY'S AWAKE TIME

The length of time your baby can be happily awake is determined by his age. A newborn is unable to cope with stimulation and interaction for the same length of time as a toddler before becoming over-stimulated. If your baby is consistently fighting his day sleeps and cries as soon as you put him down, chances are that you have simply kept him awake for too long, allowing his young brain to become over-stimulated. Chapter 6 deals with day-sleep routines and awake times in detail.

Limit the length of social outings

No outing should be longer than one hour per year of your baby's life. In other words, a one hour social visit is as much as the average one year old can manage, whilst most two year olds can cope with two hours of birthday party fun and games. If you over-socialise your baby and over-schedule him, you are likely to have a tired, grumpy or frenetic baby who may fall asleep in the evening out of sheer exhaustion, but who will not sleep peacefully throughout the night.

Ensure sufficient movement stimulation

Limiting stimulation during the day to prevent over-stimulation is important; however, there is one type of stimulation that some babies don't get enough of in order to sleep well, namely movement stimulation. It is important to have **sufficient movement** in your baby's daily activities to ensure he will sleep well. If your baby is a very placid or sedentary baby, quite happy to sit or lie still all day, or if your baby or toddler is watching too much television during the day, this lack of movement stimulation may be the reason why he is still waking at night, needing to be rocked back to sleep.

To ensure your baby is not waking for this reason, introduce two five-minute sessions of movement in the late afternoon (between 4 pm and 5 pm). Ideas for movement include:

- Swinging on a swing
- A walk around the block in a pram or sling
- Swimming for toddlers
- Pulling your six-month-old around the kitchen in a cardboard box
- A jolly jumper used for a short period under supervision
- An infant swing
- Lying in a hammock with mommy or daddy

Pay attention to proprioception

One of the reasons that exercise, such as hiking, cycling or a jogging, helps us sleep better is that **deep pressure** and **joint compression** is regulating and calming to our nervous system. We call this sensory input **proprioception** and it is vital for good sleep.

- **Swaddling** In the early days the best way to apply deep pressure is by firmly swaddling your baby with a stretchy cotton blanket. The jerky movement of his little limbs when he is sleeping comes up against the resistance of the swaddling blanket, which will prevent him from waking up.
- **Baby massage** The firm slow strokes of baby massage provide wonderful calming proprioceptive input. Massage your baby in the morning if he is younger than three months of age, as the evening is often a trying time for young babies, especially if they have not slept well during the day. The calming effect of massage lasts all day and enhances sleep in this way.

Place your baby
on the blanket

Fold up the bottom
of the blanket

Wrap one arm against
her body by bringing
one corner diagonally
across her body

Wrap the other arm in and
tuck the remaining corner
under her

- If your toddler is a sensory seeker, resists going to bed at night, and is still waking frequently at night, you will need to be sure that he is receiving enough proprioception during the day. **Play games** in the afternoon that have a strong push or pull element, such as rough and tumble games, crawling up a steep embankment or slide, hanging on monkey bars or rings, pushing a trolley loaded with heavy books – old telephone books make a wonderfully heavy load.

> SLEEP SECRET
> Recent research shows swaddling prevents spontaneous wakings in babies who are put to sleep on their back.

STIMULATION PRIOR TO BEDTIME

We know that the drowsy state precedes the sleep states. Even as adults, we use little rituals that shift us into a drowsy state at bedtime, such as drinking a cup of hot chocolate or reading a good novel. It is unrealistic, in light of this, that we expect our babies to go from a happy alert state to a sleeping state as soon we pop them into their cots. Your baby needs to shift into a drowsy state *before* he is put into his cot in order to fall asleep with ease.

Designate a period of time before each sleep to help your baby shift into a drowsy state before putting him down. During the day, watch your baby's awake

When calming your baby before sleep time, do not be concerned about 'bad habits'. Your baby needs to be calm before sleep can happen, so do what it takes to calm him down – he will not become dependent on calming measures if he is put down drowsily awake. Bear in mind that some babies need more time to get into the calm state before sleep than others, so try not to compare your baby with other babies. Trust your instinct – you will know when he is calm.

times and take him into his bedroom or sleep zone approximately **15 minutes before each day sleep**. In the evening spend at least **half an hour before bedtime** engaging in soothing activities to prepare your baby for sleep.

Once in your baby's sleep space use the following strategies to induce the drowsy state and then put your baby down into his cot:

- **Darken the room** by closing blinds or curtains during the day, and using a dimmer or passage light at night.
- **Sing** a calming lullaby (see Appendix D).
- **Rock your baby** in your arms until you see his eyelids becoming heavy and he has a slow-motion double blink, with a relaxed body and loosely opened hands – these signs indicate that he is really drowsy.
- **Do not make too much eye contact** or smile at your baby during this time if these signals alert him.
- Put **white noise** on in your baby's room to help him shift down from the calm alert state to the drowsy state quicker. In addition to making him drowsy, white noise will help your baby sleep better by filtering out any sounds that may stimulate him. White noise in the nursery can be a fan, humidifier, air conditioner, a radio tuned to no station or a recorded white-noise CD.
- **Soothing, consistent touch** is very important, whether you are feeding your baby, or simply holding him close to you. Avoid light strokes (such as tickling) as this may stimulate him and cause him to shift back into an awake and alert state. Sudden movement changes may also stimulate him, so be careful of how you handle him at this stage.

These soothing pre-sleep strategies will calm your baby into a drowsy state, which is vital for your baby to fall asleep. As soon as you see that he is in a drowsy state – NOT asleep, place him gently in his cot. Ensure that there is no rush of cold air onto his little body to alert him as he moves away from the warmth of your body (this is another reason why swaddling is so effective). As you lay him down, be sure that his head in not dipped lower than his body, as this head-first movement stimulation will alert him out of the drowsy state and you will be faced with two round eyes staring back at you! Once he is in his cot, place your whole hand (with fairly deep pressure – not tickly strokes) onto his body, and gently say 'shuuush'" for a few seconds. This will help to ease the transition from your arms to his own sleep space.

SENSORY INPUT FOR SELF-SOOTHING

Have you ever wondered why we chew on our pencil, or pull on our ear when we are trying to focus or feel a bit insecure? We all use self-initiated sensory input to help us self-soothe or regulate our states. Babies usually learn to self-regulate at the age of about nine weeks and do so by using their **mouth** or their **midline**. Your baby's extremely clever self-soothing strategies are constructive because by and large he can use them independently, which promotes good sleep habits. Your baby may use one of the following self-soothing sensory strategies to fall asleep:

- **Touch:** Your baby may touch his face or neck, hold his hands together or enjoy the feel of a soft or specific fabric or texture.
- **Mouth:** Your baby may suck his hand or fists or rely on a dummy to fall asleep. If so, he is regulating with his mouth, so encourage this if it is helping him to stay calm.
- **Vibration:** Rumour has it that when a cat gives birth, she purrs the whole way through labour! And it's not because she enjoys the pain, it's because purring creates vibration which is calming. When babies hum or moan themselves to sleep (not to be confused with crying to sleep), they are using the vibration in the voice box to self-regulate and to shift into a lower, calmer state. Sleep is not far off at this stage.

- **Movement:** Some babies and toddlers rock their heads or bang their legs against the side of the cot just before falling asleep. This does not indicate that there is something wrong – they may simply enjoy the feeling of the movement, and are using it effectively to self-calm.
- **Body position:** You may notice your baby wedging himself in the corner of the cot or always choosing a certain position to fall asleep. This position is soothing for him, and once he has attained it, he will be ready to fall asleep.

SENSORY INPUT DURING SLEEP – THE SLEEP ZONE

When last did you try to sleep on an international flight? Falling asleep is difficult enough sitting upright, but staying asleep for the whole night is near impossible. We all need a soothing sensory environment not only to fall asleep but also to stay deeply asleep.

The sensory input in your baby's sleep environment will impact on how easily he becomes drowsy in preparation for sleep, his ability to fall asleep, and whether he stays asleep. This sleep space is so important that we have dedicated an entire chapter to it (see Chapter 3: The sleep zone).

AGE-APPROPRIATE SENSORY INPUT TO SUPPORT SLEEP

In general the principles of calming sensory input are applicable to all ages; however, there are specific age-defined sensory strategies that are useful to know about.

> *SLEEP SECRET*
> *Do not worry about self-calming strategies becoming 'bad habits'. Most are socially acceptable strategies your baby needs. Follow your baby's lead and even assist him to find self-calming strategies that he can use independently.*

Your newborn's sensory needs (the first three months)

During the first three months your baby is most susceptible to over-stimulation because the filtering mechanisms in his nervous system are still so immature.

- Keep stimulation to a minimum during the day; just being alive is enough stimulation for a newborn baby, especially if your baby was premature.
- Limit awake time to 45-60 min between sleeps
- Always swaddle your new baby in a cotton stretchy blanket, which provides calming deep pressure. Swaddling also inhibits those 'drifting to sleep jerks' which may startle your baby awake.
- If your new baby cries when you are trying to settle him to sleep, wrap him tightly and rock him gently to get him drowsy again, then place him in his crib and gently place your hand on him, giving soothing deep pressure. Your newborn may **moan and wriggle** in this position for a short time, as he settles himself to sleep. By picking him up at this point you may add more stimuli that will alert him and wake him up.
- If your newborn begins to cry, pick him up re-swaddle him and rock him until drowsy and try again.
- Use a dim night light for night feeds.
- Play white-noise sound to re-enact the soothing world of the womb.

SLEEP SECRET
All young babies benefit from swaddling. If your baby appears to resist being swaddled, it is most likely due to immature reflexes when he cries, which move his arms away from his body. Persist with swaddling your baby and you will probably notice he calms. If you are completely certain that he fusses more when swaddled, wrap him under the arms.

Your older baby's sensory needs

As your baby gets older, he can cope with more stimulation during the day and learns from happy interactions with you. However, keep the sleep space consistent and calming and use calming strategies before bedtime:

- Be sure to fit in some calming time before each sleep and remember to enter the sleep zone at least 15 minutes before the awake time is up.
- Before bedtime, a soothing bath using lavender or chamomile scented bath products is a good idea. Try to keep bath time as calm as possible.
- Once your baby outgrows swaddling, wanting his hands free, wrap him under the arms.
- Keep the room dim and remove all stimuli, such as pictures on the walls and mobiles from around the cot, especially if your baby is alert and experiencing sleep difficulties.
- If your baby resists going to sleep during the day and at bedtime in the evening, you have probably let him stay awake for too long. Even though your baby is no longer a newborn, and is fascinated with his world, it is still very important to watch those awake times, which range from an hour to three by the time they turn a year old. (See Awake times, page 61.)

Your toddler's and preschooler's sensory needs

Toddlers are notoriously susceptible to over-stimulation for two reasons. Firstly, we expect so much more from them in all facets of their lives. We expose them to so many stimuli on a daily basis. They may well be at playschool by now, having an extremely busy morning, as well as an afternoon filled with outings and exciting events. This overloaded world they are exposed to results in over-stimulation.

Secondly, because of their developing movement skills, toddlers seek an enormous amount of stimulation as they go about their daily lives. They are unable to read their own internal signals when they become over-stimulated, and this invariably leads to behavioural issues and delayed bedtimes.

- Watch for signs of over-stimulation and limit social expectations by keeping each play date to an hour per year of your child's age.
- Ensure all sleeps happen in the sleep zone.
- After bath, do not leave their sleep zone and rather spend quiet time doing calming activities before bed, such as reading, doing a puzzle or playing with building blocks.
- Make sure your toddler has sufficient opportunity for movement activities during the day and is not watching too much TV. Limit TV completely for an hour or two before bed.
- Keep a night light on in your toddler's sleep zone, as their imagination develops at about 18 months old and they develop fears of being in the dark. Keep it on for the whole night, so that your toddler can recognize his sleep zone should he wake up in the night, and thus not be frightened of imaginary monsters.

SUMMARY OF SENSORY SECRETS FOR SLEEP

- Provide a **balanced sensory diet** of movement stimulation and deep pressure along with appropriate calming activities during the day.
- **Avoid over-stimulating** your baby or toddler during the day and close to bedtime in the evening, as over-stimulated children can't switch off and tend to fight sleep at night.
- Make sure that you use calming strategies to assist the **transition into the drowsy state** in preparation for sleep for at least 10 minutes before day sleeps and half an hour before bedtime in the evening
- Help your baby find **self-soothing** sensory strategies.
- Make sure your baby's **sleep space** is conducive to sleep, and use sensory calming strategies (such as white noise, or muted light) to help your baby to remain asleep and shift sleep cycles effortlessly.

STEPS TO A GOOD NIGHT'S SLEEP
1. Have appropriate expectations of your child's sleep
2. Use sensible calming strategies before and during sleeptime to improve your child's sleep.

CHAPTER 3

The sleep zone

STEP 3: YOUR BABY'S SLEEP ENVIRONMENT MUST SUPPORT SLEEP

Mike and Patty were having a real time of it with Leah. They had started off feeling that she should fit into their lifestyle and so let her sleep wherever they were. And as a young baby, Leah was a pleasure, dropping off to sleep at a restaurant or in the car. Life felt easy. Now as a 20-month-old toddler she was such a difficult child at bedtime that her parents had even moved her from her cot to a bed. Even so she fell asleep best in front of the TV, but Patty knew this wasn't the best parenting strategy so tried to get Leah to go to sleep in her own bed each night. Leah would hop out of bed instantly and throw tantrum after tantrum until eventually at ten at night, she was collapsing into an exhausted sleep on Patty's bed.

The importance of a sleep space or sleep zone that supports healthy sleep must not be underestimated. When we consult with parents about their children's sleeping issues, the lack of a suitable sleep zone is frequently the piece of the puzzle that is missing. This chapter is intended to assist you in creating an optimal sleep space for your baby within the context of your family and living conditions. As Leah's parents experienced, like most new babies Leah was blissfully unaware of where she fell asleep. But as she gets older, the space where she sleeps takes on greater significance and will play a role in helping her develop healthy sleep habits.

> *SLEEP SECRET*
> *Your baby's sleep zone needs to be conducive to sleep, to support your efforts while you work at developing good sleep habits. The hallmark features of an optimal sleep zone are: **calmness** and **consistency**.*

An inadequate sleep zone may be affecting your child's sleep if

- There is no consistency to where your baby falls asleep
- Your baby frequently will only fall asleep if she is being driven in the car or is in front of the TV
- Your baby co-sleeps with you at night, but is extremely restless, preventing a good night's sleep
- Your baby is sleeping in an area surrounded by many toys, mobiles and bright patterns in the cot.

A CONSISTENT SLEEP ZONE

In the early days your baby may have fallen asleep wherever she was, in a restaurant, in your arms in the TV room or in the car seat. Since very small babies sleep a lot, from a practical point of view it is not always possible to be in a consistent sleep zone if chores have to be done outside of the house.

You may also have liked the fact that your baby fitted in with your lifestyle;

sleeping as easily at dinner parties as she did at home in her bed. It simply made sense to you to let her sleep whenever she needed to, no matter where you might have been. Although this works in the early days, one of two scenarios may develop as your baby grows more alert and socially aware:

• Older babies are not as happy to go to sleep in a strange and busy environment, and begin to resist sleep, even when at home.
• Alternately, some babies learn to expect excitement and are not prepared to go to bed in their sleep zone when you spend an evening at home.

It is inevitable that an inconsistent sleep zone will impact negatively on healthy sleep habits. Before you know it, you have reached the toddler years, and your toddler is still falling asleep (day nap and bedtime) wherever she wants – whether it is on the couch in front of the TV, or in the back of the car as you drive around the block in a desperate attempt to get her to sleep!

If your baby is a poor sleeper it may well be because her sleep zone is inconsistent She is most likely falling asleep in one place and waking up in another. Small wonder she is restless and unhappy! It is time to choose a sleep space for your child, and to use this zone consistently. Once you have conveyed to your child 'a vote of confidence' in her sleep zone (by being consistent), you will be amazed how effective this small strategy can be.

Where should your baby's sleep zone be?

There's nothing quite like that special feeling of snuggling up in bed with your baby. A whisper of soft breath, that special baby smell, and the utter bliss of a sleeping child. For some parents, their choice is to have their babies in bed with them. In many cultures it is the accepted norm for children to share their parents' bed for many years. Indeed, in many homes, bed sharing, or room sharing is a necessity due to lack of adequate housing space or for cultural reasons. Many parents simply enjoy having their children close to them. For others, the idea of sharing a bed, let alone a bedroom, with their child is just not their scene and the reality of sharing a bed with a restless baby or toddler may result in no sleep for anyone – not an ideal situation.

Many babies start off in their parents' bed for ease of feeding and a few months down the line, dad ends up moving into another room in search of a good nights sleep. It's no wonder that many parents find that the novelty of 'all in the bed' soon wears off, and a good night's sleep for all becomes of paramount importance.

How does one choose what is best for your baby?

Co-sleeping

There is evidence that co-sleeping in the early days is a good choice. It helps your baby feel secure and regulates her breathing and body temperature. For moms it is also convenient as you can respond with ease to feeding needs at night.

Some parents do not like the idea of co-sleeping and are worried about the safety of having their baby sleeping in their bed. If you are a sensory sensitive person, the movements and noises of a little body in your bed may prevent you from having a good night's sleep.

The bottom line is that the choice is personal and either alternative works well. So in the early days choose your baby's sleep space according to your own preferences to allow you to have as much sleep as possible, so that you are well rested to feed and nurture your baby.

A sense-able option for the early weeks is to let your baby sleep next to your bed in a co-sleeper cot or her own crib. In this way, she is close enough to be heard and feeds are convenient. A co-sleeper cot is a normal cot pushed up alongside your bed with the side down. This creates an 'extension' of your bed.

Opting for a nursery

You may choose for your baby to sleep in her own room right from the start and *will* probably find that she settles in with ease. If this is your choice, rest assured that you will hear your baby when she needs you, as you are very tuned in to her sounds and cries. You might even find yourself in the nursery without being fully awake yet! If your house is very large, and you are worried about not hearing your baby, invest in a baby monitor to ensure your quick response to her cries.

Moving your young baby to her own sleep zone

Choosing to share a bed with your newborn is a common choice, but many parents find that as their baby gets older it's no longer the comfortable option. The question arises about the right time to move a baby and how to ease the transition to her own sleep space.

The following will indicate that it is time to consider moving your baby or toddler into her own sleep zone:

- Your baby is disturbing you or your partner's sleep and you are getting **less** rather than **more** sleep.
- Sleep deprivation is impacting on your emotional relationship with your baby during the day. Your being emotionally available is more beneficial for your baby than co-sleeping is. So it is very important that you are rested enough to respond to your baby.
- Just as you are disturbed by your baby's movements and sleep noises so she is probably disturbed by yours. Babies who are sensitive to touch (resist being wrapped up or cuddled with) or those who are disturbed by sounds invariably sleep better in their own rooms.

- You and your partner are no longer in agreement about your baby sleeping with you (whether it is in your bed or your room). Sharing the marital bedroom with a baby or toddler is something you need to be in agreement on.
- It is a good idea to move your baby into her own sleep space before she gets too old (before five months of age). The older she gets, the more likely it is that habits will form, as she will take comfort in familiarity. This makes the transition to her own sleep zone harder, but not impossible.
- After four months of age, nutritional support during the night has decreased significantly to only one feed at night, so as long as she is well and healthy, this is a good time to move your baby to her own sleep zone.

The move to her own nursery will be seamless before four months of age, but if you decide to co-sleep after six months of age you should make that decision for the long term or be prepared to face some resistance from her. Bear in mind also that it is unsafe to have your toddler and a newborn sleeping in your bed. It is also unfair to expect your toddler to move to her own room two days before the arrival of a new baby. So move your toddler long before you contemplate having a new baby in the bed with you. (See page 37 for those strategies.)

Moving your older baby to a nursery

If your baby or toddler has been sleeping in your bed for a while she may protest the idea of moving to her own bed. Having a strategy to follow and a goal in sight makes it much easier to focus on the long term (that will hopefully include a lot more sleep!), rather than getting caught up in the moment and losing hope of ever having a decent night's sleep! That goal is to reclaim your sleep space, and to create and encourage a calm and safe sleep zone for your child.

If you have made the decision to move your baby out of your bed and into her own sleep zone, but are feeling rather daunted at the prospect of actually *doing* it, follow the simple guidelines below. Remember that if your baby has been co-sleeping with you, it will take her (and you) time to get used to sleeping alone.

- Make sure that your baby is healthy and thriving before making any changes.
- Ensure that the new sleep zone is calming and similar to the one you are moving her from. So, whether she is moving from your bed to a crib in your room, or to her own room, keep the sensory environment the same – dimmed room, with a blanket that smells of mommy.
- Keep your calming strategies the same as they were before, but use them in the new sleep zone.
- Respond to her cries and needs once she is in her new environment to reassure you both.
- If you have been assisting her to fall asleep (whether it be rocking her or feeding her), keep doing so in her new sleep zone. Once she is used to her new space (give it about 3-4 days), you can begin to change the way she falls asleep (age-appropriate sleep coaching guidelines are found on pages 87-99).
- Expect some disturbed sleep on your part for the first few nights. You may be anxious that you are not going to hear your baby's cries. Give yourself time to get used to the new sleeping arrangements – you may well take longer to adjust than your baby does!
- If your child is already a toddler, expect more resistance but persevere!

> **SLEEP SECRET**
> No matter where you choose your baby's sleep zone to be, don't forget about the sensory environment your baby is exposed to. Keep the sleep space calm and unstimulating.

Moving your toddler from a cot to a bed

Do not be tempted to move your toddler from a cot into a bed too early. Boundaries such as staying put in her own bed are not easily understood by babies under two years old. Restless sleeping and frequent night wakings are not an indication that your baby needs to be moved. Wait until your toddler starts to make attempts to climb over the rails of her cot before moving her to a bed. This usually happens at around two years of age.

Once you have made the choice to move her, buy a good quality mattress that will see you through her childhood and invest in a side bar to prevent her falling out of bed. Position her bed against a wall or chest of drawers to prevent her from falling out of the bed in the initial period.

Buy her special linen or a sleep toy and start the transition to her new bed with the sleep for which she generally goes down easiest. Enact the exact bedtime routine you always have so that her brain is cued for sleep.

For her first time of sleeping in her bed, sit with her until she is drowsy and then say goodnight and walk out the room matter-of-factly. A good sleeper will probably drop off to sleep barely noticing the difference from her cot.

If your toddler immediately jumps out of bed as you leave the room, place her back in bed and tell her you will sit with her until she is asleep. (You may need a few sleep coaching tips from page 96.)

(You may need a few sleep coaching tips from page 96.)

A CALMING SLEEP SPACE

Having explored the importance of consistency we now look at the soothing criteria that make up a calming sleep zone. Create the optimal soothing sleep environment with these ideas:

Touch

- Use **soft brushed-cotton** or stretch-interlock sheets for your baby's bedding. Stiff cotton has a rougher feel on your baby's skin, which is not soothing.
- **Deep pressure** touch helps babies stay asleep longer but owing to the risk of suffocation and over-heating, do not use a heavy duvet. Rather wrap your baby for as long as she is happy to be swaddled. For really poor sleepers, a weighted blanket may be used. However, use this only under the guidance of a sensory integration trained occupational therapist or once your toddler is over 18 months of age.
- The optimal **temperature** for your baby's room is 20° to 22° – any hotter than this and your baby will be uncomfortable and overheat when sleeping. Invest in a good room thermometer and use a fan to cool the room down or a humidifier or panel heater to warm it to the right temperature.
- If your baby kicks off her blankets, put her in a 100% cotton baby **sleeping bag** to ensure she stays warm as the night cools down.
- Your baby's **clothes** for sleep need to be soft and 100% cotton for comfort and safety.

Sounds for sleep

- Sing soothing **lullabies** or play lullaby music in your baby's room for bedtime soothing sounds.
- **White noise**, such as a fan, humidifier, fountain outside the room or white noise CD, helps your baby to move between sleep cycles from light sleep into deep sleep without waking. In addition, white noise blocks out sound from the environment which could wake your baby.

SLEEP SECRET
The space where your baby sleeps takes on great significance as she gets older and will play a large role in helping her develop good sleep habits. **Consistency,** and a **calming sleep space** are the key to establishing a healthy sleep zone for your child.

Visual

- Keep your baby's room **dark** with block out lining on blinds for day and night sleep in the early days. The darkness helps signal to the brain to release melatonin, our sleep hormone.
- During night feeds use a passage light or **light dimmer** in the bedroom, to let you see what you are doing while keeping the environment calm and un-stimulating.
- Before imagination develops at 18 months, babies do not need night-lights. A light in her bedroom may alert your young baby during the night.
- If your baby is a poor sleeper and is older than 9 months, however, she may benefit from the comfort of a passage light to reference where she is, should she wake.
- After 18 months when imagination develops a night-light is important to quell fears of the dark and imagined bogeymen.

SUMMARY OF YOUR BABY'S SLEEP ZONE

- Make your own choice confidently about **co-sleeping** in the early days.
- For a good night's sleep, your baby's sleep zone must be **consistent** for day and night sleeps so that she associates a space with sleep. This association triggers the release of essential sleep hormones.
- Moving your baby to her own sleep zone will be easier when she is young (before four months.)
- Do not move your toddler from a **cot to her own bed** before two years of age.
- Create a **sensory calming sleep space** for your baby so that stimulation is kept to a minimum, and the release of sleep hormones is not inhibited.

> ### STEPS TO A GOOD NIGHT'S SLEEP
> 1. Make sure your expectations of your baby are appropriate
> 2. Structure your baby's sensory experiences during the day and at night to enhance sleep.
> 3. Make sure your baby's sleep zone is age-appropriate, consistent and calming.

Sound nutrition for a good night's sleep

CHAPTER 4

STEP 4: RULE OUT HUNGER AS A CAUSE OF NIGHT WAKINGS

Kyle is 9 months old and is waking up to four times at night to drink milk. Her mother, Paula, is understandably at her wits end. When Kyle was younger, he was a hungry baby who fed two-hourly day and night. Even though he is drinking milk at bedtime, he wakes every two or three hours during the night for feeds. He is not particularly interested in solid food during the day, preferring to drink milk. His mom dreads meal times, and is sure Kyle is waking hungry at night. Paula is reluctant to let him cry at night, so is continuing to feed him on demand. She knows something needs to change, but is unsure of where to even begin to get things right.

As mothers we measure our success by tangible things like weight gain, sleep and how happy our baby is. When weight gain slows or sleep is disrupted or our baby is not happy, the first thing to enter our head is 'am I meeting his nutritional needs?' In the newborn days of breastfeeding we have no idea if our baby is getting enough milk, as breasts don't come with calibration (an inconvenient truth). When our baby is a little older and wakes frequently at night we have to make the decision about when solids should be introduced. Then in the toddler years, our little ones decide that fresh air is as nutritious as the five food groups and become such fussy eaters we have no idea whether they are getting enough to eat.

It is no wonder that nutrition is the most common scapegoat for poor sleep habits in the first three years. The big question is **can nutrition be blamed** for poor sleep?

If your baby is healthy and thriving and is sleeping for age-appropriate periods of time at night without needing nutrition, you can be assured that you are on the right track.

Remember until your baby is about 6 weeks old or weighs in the region of about 5 kg, he probably won't be able to sleep for more than five hours at a time without waking with hunger. The periods of time that he can manage to go without a feed will obviously increase as your baby grows. However, if your baby is still feeding frequently at night and it is no longer age-appropriate for him to be doing so, it might be time to look at his nutritional needs to eliminate hunger as a possible cause of sleeplessness.

Hunger or nutritional needs may be affecting your child's sleep if
- He is no longer sleeping for an age-appropriate length of time at night, and will only settle if he is fed more frequently.
- The time between day feeds shortens, and he is generally unsettled
- His weight gain has slowed despite drinking milk frequently
- He displays any of the above symptoms and is older than 4 months of age, or weighs in the region of 7 kg or more
- If he is 6 months or older and is not on solids (even if not showing any of the above signs)
- He is not ill (see page 51 to exclude medical issues)

You should expect your baby to need to feed frequently in the beginning, resulting in short sleep spells. As your baby grows, you can expect an increase in the stretches of sleep. To refresh your memory about reasonable sleep stretches at night here they are again:

0-2 weeks:	Expect sleep to take place in between feeds, which will most likely be on demand. Do not expect any significantly long stretches of sleep at this stage.
2-6 weeks:	One 4-5 hour stretch between two night feeds (usually in the first part of the evening) and 2-4 hour stretches thereafter.
6-12 weeks:	One 6-7 hour stretch from bedtime to the first night feed and anything from 3-4 hour stretches thereafter.
3-6 months:	One 8-10 hour stretch from bedtime to the early hours of the morning, and then a 3-4 hour stretch thereafter.
6-12 months:	A 10-12 hour stretch from bedtime until the first early morning feed.
3-5 years old:	A 11-12 hour stretch through the night. Day sleep usually falls away around this time.

BREAST-FEEDING AND SLEEP

Breast milk is your baby's natural food. Research over many years has clearly proven the many benefits of breastfeeding, including a reduction in digestive disturbances and allergies. For this reason many moms pursue breastfeeding even when it is not something that happens as easily as expected. In the early days you expect your baby to wake at night to feed, but nine weeks down the line, when your baby is still waking at night, many moms wonder if breast milk simply is not enough and whether formula milk or solid food would help their baby sleep better.

Firstly, it is important to know that if your breast milk supply is adequate, there is no reason to think that hunger is the reason for your baby's lack of sleep.

Your milk is sufficient for your baby if:
- He is growing
- He is having 6-7 wet nappies in 24 hours
- He seems settled after a feed

Your milk supply may be low in the evening

If your baby hardly sleeps during the day or your days are very busy, you may experience a reduced milk supply which is often at its lowest at the end of the day. This is because the release of *oxytocin*, one of the milk-making hormones, is negatively influenced by your own sensory overload and exhaustion. If you have had a run of bad nights, another milk-making hormone called *prolactin*, which is stimulated by rest, will also be inhibited. This may well be the reason why your baby is hungry and wakeful.

The one solution would be to feed on demand, both day and night, in order to keep your baby fed and happy, and if this works for you, keep going!

Try to eat a balanced diet, drink plenty of fluids and rest as often as possible to keep your milk supply going. Since this is not a book on breastfeeding, the topic is not covered in great detail. It is worth investing in a good book that will guide you in the art of breastfeeding (see Appendix D).

SUPPLEMENTARY OR COMPLEMENTARY BOTTLE-FEEDING

If you have addressed the issue of breast-milk supply **or** your bottle-fed baby is finishing his entire evening bottle and still wakes more frequently at night than expected (see page 21) you may need to eliminate hunger as a reason for your baby not sleeping. When you settle your baby for the evening, try offering him a 'top-up', or **supplementary feed** of formula milk or expressed breast milk immediately after the feed to make sure he is full. You may only need to do this at his bedtime feed. If he consistently refuses this 'top up', you can safely assume that he is not hungry. Ask your clinic sister or paediatrician to advise you on a formula choice.

Complementary feeding is when a bottle of formula milk is given as a full feed on its own, where breastfeeding is the norm at other feeds. If you are busy with demands from other children or a hectic career, a complementary feed at bedtime may go a long way towards ensuring your baby is not waking from hunger in the first part of the night.

FORMULA-MILK CHOICES

If you have made the choice to bottle feed your baby, you can rest assured that with today's wide choice of milk formulas and readily available information on sterilizing of bottles and preparation of feeds, your baby will be well fed. Infant feeds have advanced significantly over the last decade, and there are certain formulas available for specific digestive disturbances (see page 53) and for *hungry* babies. If your baby is not on the most age-appropriate nutrient-dense formula available, change to one of them to see if it will help. Ask your clinic sister or paediatrician for guidance in choosing the correct one.

> SLEEP SECRET
> Demand feeding in the early weeks is important to establish an adequate milk supply. In the long run, unrestrained demand feeding does not allow your baby to learn to self-soothe, something we know is vital to instil healthy sleep habits.

SOLID FOOD AND SLEEP

It is understandable that young babies need to feed often during the day and night. But when your baby is between four and seven months old and still waking frequently to feed, you will find yourself wondering whether he is waking because he is hungry. There are two relevant stages in which nutritional needs change.

- Until four to six months of age, milk alone in the right quantities will probably meet your baby's nutritional needs. However, in time, milk alone may not meet his kilojoule and energy requirements to allow him to continue to grow and sleep for periods of time without feeding. This prompts the first change of diet: **from milk alone to introducing limited solid food**.

- Essential fatty acids are the building blocks of brain development. After your baby turns 6 months, milk alone no longer supplies all these vital fatty acids and a new form of protein becomes essential in your baby's diet. This is when the diet changes **from milk and basic solids such as vegetables to include protein**.

Introducing solids

There is no set time, or any rules about introducing solids to your baby, unless he suffers from severe allergies, or if your family is very allergy-prone.If this is the case, it may be advisable to wait until he is six months old. If there is no risk of allergies, it is best to be guided by his feeding and sleeping pattern, and body mass. If your baby is not sleeping well, is between four and six months of age and you think he may be ready for solids, follow this simple guide:

STEP ONE

Begin with a **single grain** baby cereal (rice **or** maize) as an evening meal. Mix a heaped teaspoon of the dry cereal with expressed breast milk, formula or cooled, boiled water to make a sloppy mixture. Offer it to your baby between 4 and 5 pm. Gradually increase the amount you give him each day, and adjust the consistency to suit his taste. If he is younger than 5 months, this may be all he needs at this stage to provide him with extra fuel for the night. If he is older than 5 months, continue for two weeks, then move to step two.

STEP TWO

At about 8 am, offer him the same amount of cereal that he is having in the evening. Continue with cereal in the morning and evening for one week. If he is younger than five months, wait for him to show you that he is hungry before adding this step – if he is still waking at night, or does not manage to last to three to four hours after his early morning feed.

STEP THREE

After he has been on two cereal meals of per day for one week, substitute the evening cereal with vegetables. Stick to vegetables with yellow or orange flesh (carrots, pumpkin, baby marrow, butternut, sweet potato), boiled or steamed and pureed with no extra salt or sugar and moistened with a little breast or formula milk if necessary. If your baby is younger than five months, give him cereal in the morning and vegetables in the evening until he shows signs of needing a third meal (see step 4). If he is older than five months continue with step 3 for a week, then move to step 4.

STEP FOUR

If he remains hungry at night, or becomes hungry and unsettled around lunchtime (by demanding more milk at around noon) move on to this step. Offer him pureed fresh, raw fruit (banana, pear, papaya, avocado pear, mango melon or steamed apples) at this time. Do not add extra sugar, but if necessary moisten with breast or formula milk.

By now, your baby will be on three solid meals a day, but his milk feeds remain the same (approximately four-hourly). Continue with this meal plan for a further two weeks.

STEP FIVE

Introduce one tablespoon of natural yoghurt into one meal of the day. Either mix it into his cereal, or add it to fresh fruit, or give it separately after vegetables. Continue with this diet until your baby is at least six months old. Do not give him proteins such as meat, poultry, cheese, eggs or fish yet. At this stage solid food must in no way take the place of milk feeds. Remember that solids are given **in addition to** breast or formula milk. Mix into porridge, or add to fruit, or give after veggies. He will now be eating or drinking something roughly every two hours. This will keep his blood sugar levels stable, and will eliminate hunger during the day. Depending on your baby's body mass and age, he should be able to last up to ten hours at night without needing a feed.

Time	Feeding guideline at five to six months
6 am	Milk feed (breast or formula)
8 am	Breakfast: Baby cereal or fruit
10 am	Milk feed (breast or formula)
12 noon	Fruit or vegetables
2 pm	Milk feed (breast or formula)
4-5 pm	Dinner: Baby cereal or vegetables
6-7 pm	Milk feed (breast or formula)
EXPECT A STRETCH OF EIGHT TO TEN HOURS SLEEP AT NIGHT	
2-5 am or after 2 am	Milk feed (breast or formula)

General notes on solid foods

- Offer your baby solids when he is in a good mood, not when he is screaming for milk, or is dog-tired.
- Respect his moods and feelings. Just as we have days when we don't feel very hungry, so do babies.
- Try not to let meal times become an issue between you and your baby.
- Don't force-feed your baby. This could result in vomiting after five minutes.
- Introduce a single new food at a time, about two to three times in a row, before moving on.
- Generally, time the feed to about one to two hours after a milk feed (which is also one to two hours before a milk feed)
- If your baby is sleeping, don't wake him up for a meal – rather delay it by an hour or skip it altogether
- Invest in a hand-held blender; it will be very useful for a long time to come.

NUTRITION AND OLDER BABIES

Once your baby is six months old, his nutritional needs change once again. His growing body needs more than milk to supply him with constant energy to keep him content during the night. The emphasis now moves from milk as the sole source of nutrition, to an increasing need for solid food. If your baby has been on milk feeds only, and is healthy, thriving and sleeping for age-appropriate lengths of time at night without needing nutritional support, you can count yourself lucky! However, now is the time to introduce some solid food if you have not done so already. Your baby is sitting up, reaching out and is really interested in his world, so he is more than ready to experience something new and exciting! It is important to expose him to different tastes and textures in his mouth at this stage to prevent fussy eating habits developing later on.

Your baby now needs **protein** in his diet. Protein builds healthy bones and tissue, and is vital for the growth and development of all children. Protein is nutrient-dense and carries the essential fatty acids, the building blocks of brain development, which our body cannot produce. Furthermore, protein alleviates hunger, so this may well be the reason that your *healthy* baby is still waking at night needing feeds. It is important to ensure that his pre-sleep meal supplies sufficient energy to keep him asleep, as well as a good balance of protein, carbohydrates and fats. If your baby is on formula milk, change to a formula specifically for babies aged six months and older. This milk contains more protein and fat and will cater for his growing needs.

How much protein does my baby need?

Your baby's **minimum** protein requirement in a 24-hour period is approximately: 1 g (equivalent to one teaspoon) of protein per kilogram of body weight. Your baby at six months of age most likely weighs in the region of 7-9 kilograms, so this means so he will need a minimum of 7-10 teaspoons of protein per day, divided up into his three meals. This would mean 2-4 teaspoons of protein per meal on an average day. Another simple way of estimating his protein need for the meal is to make it the size of the palm of his hand.

Both animal protein (dairy products, meat, poultry and fish) and vegetable protein (legumes, beans and seeds – ground or in paste form) are suitable. For recipe ideas consult Annabel Karmel's **New complete baby and toddler meal planner.** (Random House 2004.)

If your child is recovering from an illness and is simply not eating solid food at all, it is a good idea to add a specialized powdered protein supplement to his bedtime milk to get him back on track. Ask your clinic sister or paediatrician to recommend a suitable one.

> If you have a family history of allergies, or your baby shows signs of allergies, certain proteins such as dairy, nuts, fish, soya and eggs should be avoided until your baby is at least one year old. It is advisable to seek expert advice with regard to a hypoallergenic diet.

Carbohydrates

Another important source of energy for our bodies is found in carbohydrates, which should be included in every meal. Examples of suitable carbohydrates are:

• cereals and grains
• potato
• pasta
• orange vegetables, peas and corn

Try not to give your baby refined carbohydrates such as white bread and processed foodstuffs. Fibre that is found in grains (such as barley or oats) is important to assist slow, continuous absorption of nutrients into the blood stream. Fibre also assists with the gradual release of glucose (sugar) into the bloodstream to provide the necessary energy to stay full. This slow release of carbohydrates also prevents sugar spikes. These sugar spikes may be contributing to a baby's wakefulness or a toddler's irritability. The latest research indicates that the best way to produce a feeling of fullness and reduce sugar spikes is to include a protein such as meat, poultry, fish and breast or formula milk with a carbohydrate.

The importance of iron

Iron is a vital component of haemoglobin (our red blood cells). It is these red blood cells that transport oxygen to our vital organs to ensure optimal health. Iron is also important to assist your baby's motor development. An iron deficiency may cause frequent night wakings (see page 54); it is therefore important to include plenty of green leafy vegetables in your baby's diet as well as an adequate intake of red meat. Because most babies do not eat enough iron-rich foodstuffs, it is recommended that your baby take a daily iron supplement to keep him healthy.

Ask your clinic sister or pharmacist to recommend one for you. Include Vitamin C-rich foods such as fruit and orange vegetables in your baby's diet to help with the uptake of iron in his body.

Vitamins, minerals and fats

- Vitamins and minerals are essential co-factors in the metabolism of fats, carbohydrates and proteins. They are therefore essential for your baby's healthy growth and development.
- Vitamin C is found in broccoli, peas, tomatoes, sweet potato, cauliflower, citrus (suitable for toddlers only).
- Vitamin E is found in nuts and seeds, avocado, wheatgerm, sweet potato, beans and fish.
- Selenium is found in cottage cheese, egg, poultry, noodles, beef liver and tuna fish.
- Zinc is found in fish, oats, brown rice, baked potato, nuts and lamb.

These foods all assist in building a **healthy immune system** to prevent frequent childhood illnesses, which may contribute to wakeful nights.

Calcium is vital for bone and teeth formation. Calcium also assists *tryptophan*, an amino acid (a building block of protein), to be converted into serotonin and melatonin which are essential **brain chemicals to assist sleep**. Look out for certain baby cereals and porridges that are fortified with *tryptophan*. Other healthy sources of *tryptophan* are peanut butter, chicken, lentils, chick peas and dairy products. Sources of calcium include milk, yogurt, oats, soya and rice.

Magnesium is a very important mineral to assist sleep. Magnesium helps to promote **muscle relaxation**, and if given as a counterpart with calcium, slows down the release of the stimulatory hormones *adrenaline* and *nor-adrenalin*, which may make your baby feel stressed and wakeful. Good sources of magnesium include beans, nuts, kidney beans, banana, squash, raisins, potato skin and green peas. If your toddler wakes frequently at night complaining of sore legs, ask your pharmacist to recommend a calcium and magnesium supplement to help his muscles relax. Magnesium is also good for constipation as it has a natural laxative effect.

Fats (especially in a poly-unsaturated form) are an important dietary source to promote healthy brain, skin and joint function, and assist with energy release to keep your baby feeling full. Healthy sources of fat include fish, nuts and seeds. Your child needs plenty of fat in his diet (not junk food!), so do not give him skim milk or fat free dairy products if he is younger than five years old.

Time	Feeding guideline for older babies (up to 12 months)
6 am	Breast/formula feed
8 am Breakfast	Baby cereal or cooked oats, maize meal, Taystee Wheat, Maltabella, or millet porridge plus breast or formula milk and two to three teaspoons of protein (cottage cheese, yoghurt, egg yolk, ground almonds) OR Bread with egg OR Fresh fruit, yoghurt and ground almonds or pureed dates

Time	Feeding guideline for older babies (up to 12 months)
10 am	Boiled water, or diluted fruit juice (1t mixed with 50 ml water) or rooibos tea and a snack such as a finger biscuit
12 noon: Lunch	Avocado pear, fresh fruit and cottage or cream cheese OR Bread with egg OR Vegetable soup with bread OR Fresh fruit, yoghurt or custard with almonds, pumpkin or sesame seeds OR Mashed potato with cheese sauce, sprinkled with ground almonds or sesame seeds OR Corn rice or brown rice with creamed spinach or cheese sauce OR Bean casserole OR Chicken broth and vegetables
2 pm	Breast/formula feed
3-4 pm	Something to drink if thirsty, and a finger food for entertainment
5 pm: Dinner	Any of the lunch ideas listed above. Avoid beans as they may cause wind, which may contribute to wakefulness.
6-7 pm	Bedtime routine, which will include a bath, last milk feed (breast or formula), then bed! See page 74 for age-appropriate bedtime routines.

NUTRITION AND YOUR TODDLER

Don't be alarmed if your toddler appears to become a picky or poor eater. His growth rate slows down dramatically after the age of one, so his energy requirements do diminish, even though he is so active! There is no special diet required for toddlers. Most of the time they can eat what the rest of the family is eating, but remember to stick to the principle of a varied diet that includes proteins, carbohydrates and fats, as well as a variety of fruit and vegetables. To ensure adequate growth and development, offer your toddler in the region of 500 ml (2 cups) of milk per day given as a drink on its own, or included into his solid food. This may be fresh, full cream milk, or any of the many toddler formula milks available. Offer milk upon waking in the morning and again at bedtime in the evening. Drinking milk between meals or at night will affect your toddler's appetite, so rather offer him water or diluted fruit juice if he is thirsty during the day, and water at night.

Frequent milk feeds

You can bet that if your toddler is a poor sleeper, he will be tired and grumpy during the day. Eating a meal will be the last thing he will feel like doing. Resist the temptation (to make *you* feel better) of offering your toddler milk instead of meals during the day simply "so that he has at least got something in his tummy". If you offer him a bottle as a calming measure every time he is fussing during the day, it will set a pattern for the night too when he will expect a feed in order to go back to sleep.

SLEEP SECRET
If you have not done so already, it is a good idea to start your toddler on a multivitamin syrup that has additional iron. His intake of iron-fortified formula and foodstuffs has either lessened or stopped altogether now. This, coupled with the fact that his eating habits are rather erratic at this stage, may lead to iron-deficiency anaemia, a common cause of restless nights. Ask your pharmacist or clinic sister to recommend a suitable one.

If your toddler is still waking at night and will only go back to sleep after drinking a bottle of milk, you can be sure that, at this age, his wakefulness is **not** caused by hunger, but rather habit or a need to suck. See page 134 for age-appropriate strategies to stop night bottles.

Assess your toddler's food intake over a week and keep a food diary. You will be pleasantly surprised at how much he is really eating once you add up all the bits and bites.

SUMMARY OF NUTRITION FOR SLEEP

- Take measures to build up your milk supply if your breastfed baby is waking more frequently than three hourly at night (under four months of age).
- Offer a top-up feed after the last feed of the day to ensure your baby is not hungry when going to bed.
- Wait for your baby to show signs of hunger before introducing solids.
- Do not replace milk feeds with solids if he is younger than six months.
- Do not leave him on milk alone if he is older than six months.
- Do not replace meals with milk if he is older than a year.
- Provided your baby is not ill, night feeds are not necessary after the age of six months.
- Adequate protein in your baby's diet is necessary to eliminate hunger if he is older than six months.
- Iron supplementation is necessary for babies who were born prematurely and for all babies older than six months.

STEPS TO A GOOD NIGHT'S SLEEP
1. Your expectations of your baby's sleep are appropriate.
2. You are watching his sensory load during the day.
3. You have a consistent calming sleep zone.
4. You are meeting your baby's age-appropriate nutritional needs.

Medical causes of night wakings

CHAPTER 5

STEP 5: ELIMINATE HEALTH ISSUES AFFECTING SLEEP

Michaela's mother Heather knew there was something wrong with her baby. She had always been a good sleeper and had learnt to self-soothe at a young age. Everything was going well until a few days ago. Michaela started to wake frequently at night crying for no apparent reason. She had been grumpy during the day too, had a stuffy nose and had been feverish on and off for a few days. When she went off her food, Heather knew she must be ill. Sure enough, a visit to the doctor revealed that Michaela had an ear and throat infection. He prescribed some medication to make her well again, and after a few more sleepless nights and lots of extra cuddles and love, Michaela soon settled back into her old routine and the crisis was over.

> ### CAUTION
> This chapter is not intended to take the place of your doctor's advice. Before giving any medication to your baby, speak to your doctor, clinic sister or pharmacist.

Michaela's mom trusted her instincts and knew that something was wrong because Michaela was displaying behaviour that was not **typical** of her, both during the day and at night. If your baby has been giving you some bad nights, whether her sleeping pattern has deteriorated rapidly or if it has been a slow, insidious decline, you will be wondering if she is healthy. Obviously, if your baby is ill you will want to respond to her need for comfort while she is not feeling well. Then, of course, you will need to address her illness to ensure she recovers as quickly as possible. At this point her sleep may well return to normal.

HEALTH ISSUES?

Health issues could well be affecting your child's sleep if she
- Is crying or fussing more than normal
- Has a temperature or rash
- Is vomiting or has diarrhoea
- Has lost her appetite
- Is unusually listless or quiet
- Is on medication
- Has been recently hospitalized
- Is waking repeatedly during the night, crying, *as a new behaviour*
- Shows an abrupt change in behaviour and temperament
- Has experienced any trauma (such as a bump on the head) in the last 12 hours.

You must seek medical advice if your baby is displaying any of these symptoms.

ACUTE MEDICAL ISSUES THAT WILL AFFECT SLEEP

One of the less pleasant realities of parenting is that your happy, calm baby will probably fall ill at some stage of her life. These difficult times will undoubtedly wreak havoc with your baby's sleeping patterns. Any acute medical issue **must** be treated effectively with medical intervention before you can expect your baby's sleep to return to normal. Common acute medical conditions include:

- Upper respiratory-tract infections such as ear and throat infections and sinusitis
- Lower respiratory-tract infections such as bronchiolitis, croup and pneumonia
- Urinary-tract infections
- Encephalitis or meningitis
- Gastroenteritis (diarrhoea and vomiting)
- Any trauma or injury
- Severe nappy rash.

ONGOING ORGANIC ISSUES THAT AFFECT SLEEP

Other underlying, ongoing medical issues may also affect your baby's sleep. Your baby may not be acutely ill, but you might notice that her sleeping habits get **progressively** worse over a period of weeks and you get the feeling that something is **just not right**. You may be tempted to follow generic advice and take control by implementing some sleep-training strategies, but before you do that, we would advise you to rule out the following possible medical causes of **ongoing** sleep problems:

Gastro-oesophageal reflux

If your baby has gastro-oesophageal reflux (GOR), it may be a contributing factor to her lack of sleep. GOR is caused by an underdeveloped valve between your baby's stomach and her oesophagus (the food pipe to her stomach). This valve will strengthen with age, but meanwhile the acidic content of her stomach (milk) is constantly being regurgitated into the oesophagus. This may cause extreme discomfort, and in come cases excessive possetting (regurgitating curdled milk) or even projectile vomiting. In severe cases, it may even interfere with her ability to feed well, which in turn may affect her growth and development. Generally, though, there is nothing to worry about, provided she is thriving and gaining weight. Most babies outgrow GOR by the age of about seven months. Surgery is sometimes required, but fortunately this is uncommon. Your baby may have reflux if she

- Resists lying flat to go to sleep, especially after a feed
- Is happiest when held in the upright position
- Swallows and gags more than normal
- Is a fussy feeder
- Possets frequently and/or has frequent projectile vomiting.

SOME TIPS TO GET YOU THROUGH THIS DIFFICULT TIME

- Reflux is hard to manage while it lasts but take comfort in the knowledge that it will pass with time.
- Feed in a quiet sensory environment. Over-stimulation increases the likelihood of possetting.
- Keep your baby upright after a feed, and handle her gently (avoid vigorous winding).
- Raise the head of your baby's cot mattress with a wedge.
- Don't worry if you have to hold your baby in the upright position to sleep – you can't spoil her at this young age. Assist her in any way to achieve sleep, even if it means holding her. Try to put her into her bed when she is comfortable.
- Once she is sleeping, use white noise to help her sleep a little deeper.
- Research suggests that *increased* acidity in the stomach, which may aggravate GOR, may be due to a ph imbalance. This imbalance is due to decreased levels of good bacteria in the stomach, which are essential for healthy gut function to prevent digestive disturbances such as lactose sensitivity and candida, which may make GOR worse. If your baby was born by caesarean section, or she has been exposed to antibiotics (even through your breast milk), there is a chance that some of these good bacteria have been destroyed. Ask your pharmacist for a suitable **pro-biotic medication** to give to your baby to restore healthy gut function.
- If you are breastfeeding, cut out dairy from your diet for a week to see if that helps. If you are using formula, try a lactose-free or soy variety.
- There are special anti-reflux formulas available, so if your baby is drinking formula milk, ask a health-care provider to recommend one for you to try, or to advise you on alternate methods of thickening your baby's milk to prevent regurgitation.
- If you suspect that your baby may have reflux, speak to your paediatrician about special medication available to neutralize the acid levels in her stomach.

Glue ear

Glue ear differs from an *ear infection* and is not an acute medical issue, but rather a lingering condition, which can cause sleep difficulties. Glue ear results from undrained ear canals, which may have become filled with fluid or mucus after a head cold. They are not infected at this point. If the mucus is thick and *glue-like* (hence the name glue-ear), it will not drain through the narrow tube that drains your ear canal into your throat. When your baby lies flat (when you want her to sleep), this 'glue' causes pressure to build up in her middle ear, causing pain and irritation. This may well be a possible cause of your baby's poor sleeping patterns, especially if she wakes up crying frequently during the night.

If you think this may be contributing to sleep disruptions, see your doctor who will check your baby's ears and prescribe medication to decrease the swelling in the tube and thus allow the middle ear to drain.

Enlarged tonsils or adenoids

Enlarged tonsils or adenoids could cause your child to snore while she is sleeping. Research has shown that snoring infants sleep one and a half hours less, and wake twice as often as infants who do not snore. Your child may sleep with her mouth open and appear to have laboured breathing. Enlarged tonsils and adenoids may cause partial airway obstruction in some children during sleep, which results in very light sleep and frequent wakings. These frequent wakings are the body's protective mechanisms to ensure that your baby continues to breath.

If you notice that your child sleeps with her mouth open, has laboured breathing and wakes frequently during the night, she may have enlarged tonsils or adenoids. Consult with your paediatrician who will determine the severity of the problem and refer you to an ear nose and throat specialist, if necessary.

Worms

Once your baby becomes mobile and is exploring your home and garden more freely, she is susceptible to parasitic worm infection. The most common (and luckily the least harmful) worm that children are affected by is the *pinworm*. Infestation of the *pinworm* in your child's intestine can cause her to be a restless sleeper, as the female worm lays thousands of eggs around the anus at night (they are microscopic, so you won't be able to see them). These worm eggs can cause severe itching around the anal area. If your child is infected, she may wake up crying at night due to this irritation. She will most likely be unable to tell you what is bothering her, or be able to scratch her anus due to the presence of her nappy, and will simply cry. Take the following steps is you suspect that your child may be infected:

- It is safe to de-worm your child from one year of age. Ask your pharmacist to recommend a suitable remedy.
- Remember that the whole family (including your pets, as they may harbour other parasites too) must be treated.
- Get into the healthy habit of repeating the treatment every six months.
- At bath time every night, scrub your toddlers fingernails with a nail brush (worm eggs thrive under nails!)
- Wash your pets frequently, as their fur can harbour infective eggs.

Iron-deficiency anaemia

You may wonder what on earth a low iron count has to do with frequent night wakings.

Iron is a vital component of haemoglobin, which is found in our body's red blood cells. It is these red blood cells that transport oxygen and carbon dioxide to and from the cells in our body. Oxygen is vital for our survival, particularly the healthy function of our body's vital organs (such as our brain and our heart), without which we cannot survive. There is a theory that when your baby is asleep (particularly the deep sleep state), she breathes in less oxygen because she is breathing slowly and shallowly. If there is already a depleted state of oxygen in her body due to an iron deficiency, her vital organs may begin to show signs of stress. The brain will recognize this stress, and will wake the body up, so that a nice, big deep breath can be taken to restore oxygen levels to normal. This may happen at frequent intervals during the night.

Possible reasons for iron deficiency anaemia include
- prematurity
- chronic infection
- an exclusive milk diet after six months of age (full-term babies are born with enough iron to last them for six months – thereafter they need to get their iron from foodstuffs and supplements)
- nutritional deficiency (for example vegetarian diets)
- underlying pathology such as blood disorders or cancer
- chronic blood loss due to intestinal parasites (whipworm).

Your child may be suffering from iron-deficiency anaemia if she
- is waking frequently at night
- was premature
- looks pale and listless
- has dark smudges under her eyes
- tires easily and sleeps excessively
- is frequently ill
- has no appetite
- displays behavioural problems.

If you suspect that your child is anaemic, speak to your paediatrician, clinic sister or pharmacist to prescribe an iron supplement. Vitamin C is necessary for iron to be absorbed by the body, so it is always a good idea to put your child on a multivitamin syrup that contains vitamin C. Treatment should be ongoing until the underlying cause of the anaemia is clear, but at least an 8-10 week treatment course on an iron supplement should be completed.

CAUTION

Keep iron supplement medication safely locked away

Itching related to dermatitis or eczema

If your child has sensitive skin and is prone to rashes and itches, this may contribute greatly to restless nights. Dermatitis and eczema simply means that your child's skin is irritated because it is dry and itchy. It may also be red and scaly, sometimes with little blisters or thickened skin. It's not hard to guess that this will cause her to be very unhappy, especially at night. Most dermatitis is caused by sensitivity to detergent or skin products, occurring in an individual who has an underlying predisposition, for example in Atopic Eczema which may occur if there is a family history of allergies such as asthma or allergic rhinitis.

HINTS TO HELP EASE YOUR BABY'S DISCOMFORT

- Rinse your baby's clothes well to remove detergents and fabric softeners.
- Avoid the use of soap, rather wash your baby with aqueous cream.
- Avoid bubble baths, and perfumed baby products.
- Add soluble bath oil (not baby oil) to your baby's bath water – it 'moisturises' the water.
- Avoid wool or synthetic fabrics next to the skin – try to dress your baby in 100% cotton clothing. The same applies to her bedding.
- Avoid over-heating your baby – it will make the itching worse.
- After a bath, dry your baby well.
- Keep the skin well hydrated with appropriate body moisturisers (ask your pharmacist for advice).
- Be prepared for this to be a long-term condition that needs ongoing management.
- In severe cases your doctor may prescribe an anti-histamine to reduce itching.

Teething

It is so easy to blame teeth for bad sleeping habits that never seem to go away. Keep your wits about you and learn some 'teething savvy' to help you through this unavoidable stage of your baby's development.

- Accept that teething is a normal part of your baby's development. You (and your baby) may be lucky and sail through the teething stage, or there may be some seriously wobbly days (and nights).
- Do not confuse normal developmental milestones (such as chewing on fingers and hands, and blowing bubbles) with teething. Just before three months of age, your little one will discover her hands and chew excessively on them, creating plenty of drool and bubbles.
- Teething, by definition, is when the actual tooth cuts through the gum and appears in your baby's mouth. On average, most babies cut their first tooth at around seven months.
- This actual 'cutting' may be preceded by a period of discomfort (which may last weeks) as the teeth settle into the gums and prepare to start pushing upwards. This is usually when your baby drools excessively, and loves to chew and bite down on objects. This period of discomfort is seldom characterized by fever, loss of appetite and other illness such as diarrhoea and earache.
- Restless nights may occur when your baby is actually cutting teeth and cause you to revert to desperate measures to get your baby back to sleep such as offering 'long forgotten bottles', or bringing your baby into your bed. Avoid this temptation.

Signs that your baby may be ready to cut her first tooth include the following:
- Excessive drooling and biting down on objects
- Loss of appetite, especially sucking on the breast or bottle
- A low-grade fever, or short periods of intense fever
- A red and spotty rash around her mouth

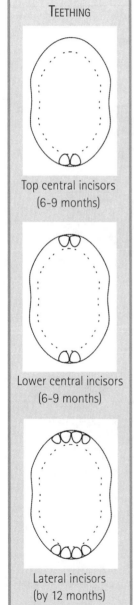

TEETHING

Top central incisors
(6-9 months)

Lower central incisors
(6-9 months)

Lateral incisors
(by 12 months)

- Nappy rash – may be severe
- Frequent, loose stools
- A runny nose
- Ear ache

If your baby is showing these signs, consult your doctor to rule out any other illness before assuming she is teething.

MANAGING TEETHING

If your child is feeling unwell while teething, treat her with teething medication that is available from your pharmacy. She may have a headache, and have a sore mouth, especially with eating. If your nights are becoming difficult, medicate with the prescribed medication at bedtime, and repeat the dose at prescribed intervals during the night if needs be.

Store your baby's dummies and teethers in the fridge – the coolness helps to soothe inflamed gums.

The effects of medication on sleep

Medication your baby is taking may have a disruptive effect on her sleep. All medication has the potential to cause side effects. These side effects range from simple symptoms like nausea, diarrhoea or vomiting, headaches, dizziness, loss of appetite, joint pain and excessive sleepiness to something more serious such as changes in heart rate. Every side effect has the possibility to cause your baby's sleeping patterns to change dramatically. Always read the package insert of any medication you are giving your child, and don't be shy to quiz your doctor or pharmacist about possible side effects of the medication they are prescribing for your child.

The effect of hospitalization on sleep

If your baby has been ill enough to have been hospitalized, and has undergone invasive or painful procedures whilst in this unfamiliar environment, this will impact greatly on her sleep. Hospitalization affects sleep for a variety of reasons not the least of which is the period of separation from you. Even if you were able to stay with your child most of the time, you may have had to leave her alone on occasion in a strange and scary environment. This could cause a state of heightened separation anxiety, particularly if the timing coincides with the known crisis periods of separation anxiety (seven to ten months and the toddler years).

Hospitals are noisy and intrusive places, so if your baby is used to sleeping in a quiet and calm environment, she will struggle to settle easily. She may become very dependent on you for soothing, even if she was able to effectively self soothe beforehand. Expect your baby to still need you to calm her for a period of time after she returns home.

The invasive and sometimes painful procedures she may have experienced in hospital frequently sensitize your baby to touch on her skin (for example intravenous lines) and around the mouth (for example nebulizing or forcing down medicine). This hypersensitivity results in heightened irritability and less use of self-soothing techniques, especially around the mouth. This is why your baby may appear to have 'gone off' her dummy or bottle as an effective soother. Be patient, and in time your baby will return to her old self.

MANAGING THE EFFECT OF HOSPITALIZATION

- As far as possible, within reason, stay with your baby in hospital.
- Keep your baby's security object or sleep soother with her at all times.
- Hold your baby and talk to her during invasive procedures so that you minimize the stress she may be feeling.
- Try to keep her hospital routine as similar as possible to that at home. If at all possible, ask the nursing staff to perform procedures in her awake times and to leave her undisturbed if she is sleeping.
- When you return home, expect and allow for a period of clinginess and sleep disruption.
- From the first night home re-implement the bedtime routine (see Chapter 7).
- As soon as she is well, encourage self-calming strategies such as a sleep soother.
- Allow her a week to ten days to settle on her own (which she is likely to do), but if she is still not settling independently, you may have to commence with age-appropriate sleep coaching (see Chapter 9).

SUMMARY OF HEALTH ISSUES AFFECTING SLEEP

- If your baby's sleep has gradually disintegrated and she is unsettled at night for a period of time you will want to rule out **chronic health issues**, such as glue ear, worms and iron deficiency.
- **Reflux** causes disruptions especially in young babies and if your baby is unsettled and never sleeping for long periods you need to rule this out.
- Beware of blaming long-term sleep issues on teething. **Teething** only really affects your baby's sleep for a few nights when she cuts teeth.
- **Acute illnesses** or periods of **hospitalization** wreak havoc with sleep and sleep issues need to be addressed once your baby is well.
- If your baby is a poor sleeper and on **medication** of any type, ask your doctor or pharmacist if the medication can affect sleep.

STEPS TO A GOOD NIGHT'S SLEEP

1. You have realistic expectations of your baby's sleep.
2. You have introduced sensory calming activities.
3. Your baby has a consistent and calming zone for sleep.
4. You have ruled out hunger and nutritional needs as a cause of night wakings.
5. You are certain no medical issues are causing night wakings.

Day-sleep routine

CHAPTER 6

STEP 6: ESTABLISH A HEALTHY DAY-SLEEP ROUTINE FOR HEALTHY NIGHT SLEEP

At nine months, Sebastian was a cutey. He endeared himself to all who met him but his mom was exhausted. This little live-wire was never still and he did not sleep at all during the day, despite being tired and crabby at times. He resisted sleep when his mom tried to get him to sleep during the day. If she was lucky enough to get him to sleep he would only cat nap if he was in the pram or the car. His mom was sure that after being awake all day he should sleep soundly at night, but Sebastian had different plans. He usually resisted bedtime, and would fall into an exhausted slumber after a fight. Then he would be awake before midnight, and his mom would have to feed or rock him to sleep once more. This pattern repeated itself throughout the night, sometimes hourly. Sebastian's mom was exhausted and at her wits end. To deal with this busy little boy all day, his mom needed sleep and she was not getting any at this rate!

If your baby has no order to his day you may find that day sleep times are a real battle. If he sleeps at unpredictable times and most of these sleeps are cat naps, he probably won't be sleeping too well at night either. A flexible routine is important and will aid the development of good sleep habits. Keep in mind that in the first **six weeks** of your baby's life he will be relatively unpredictable, as it will take him a while to develop his own routine.

Day sleep issues must be addressed if your child

- Rarely sleeps during the day
- Fights every going to sleep - day and night
- Wakes repeatedly at night
- Is fractious and irritable when awake, but especially so in the late afternoon
- Is a poor eater
- Has behavioural issues.

NATURAL SLEEP RHYTHMS

A differentiated day-night sleep cycle every 24 hours or the **circadian rhythm** as it is known, develops in your baby within the first few months of life. As the evening approaches, the pineal gland in the brain releases *melatonin*, a sleep hormone, and your baby becomes drowsy and ready to sleep.

Day/night reversal is common in newborns, as very young babies may not yet have established their 'sleep clock' or circadian rhythm. If your newborn is awake and feeding more frequently at night, but is sleeping all day, try these strategies to change his existing sleep/wake cycle:

- Keep his sensory environment and his sleep zone quiet and calming.
- Wake him up for feeds **at least** four hourly during the day, even if he is sleeping soundly.
- Do your best to keep him awake for his feed, by unwrapping him, exposing his feet, wiping his face with a damp cloth and tickling his cheek.
- At night, keep the lights low and interactions with him to a minimum during night feeds.
- Persist with this for a few days, and before long he will develop a regular/ differentiated day-night sleep cycle.

In addition to circadian rhythms, we also experience shorter internal rhythms, called **ultradian rhythms**, which are experienced every few hours. These rhythms tell us when we are hungry but also when we have dips in our wakefulness. Have you ever experienced that drowsiness after lunch? That represents your natural dip in energy and if you put your head down you could easily have a cat-nap. Most adults' natural sleep rhythms are eight hours of sleep at night and ideally, a nap in the early afternoon. For most of us, this nap does not happen, so we push on into the afternoon, but we are not as productive as we are when we are fresh in the morning. Being adults, we have adapted to cope with this dip, but your baby or toddler's dips are more frequent and he will be miserable if he does not sleep in the day.

Once night feeds are no longer required (from six months of age), your baby's natural rhythm is to sleep for 10-12 hours at night, in addition to regular day naps. These age-determined day naps are dictated by your baby's ultradian rhythms that will obviously change over time, as he gets older. We call these periods **awake times** and they are the age appropriate time spans that your baby can be happily awake before he needs to sleep again.

An **awake time** is the time from when your baby wakes until he should go down for his next sleep. All care-giving activities (feeding, bathing, nappy change), play and stimulation must take place during this time. Awake times for young babies are very short and it may surprise you how soon your baby must go back to sleep. For instance, a four week old who wakes from a nap at 10 am must go back to sleep at 10:45 am. That is literally time for a feed and nappy change.

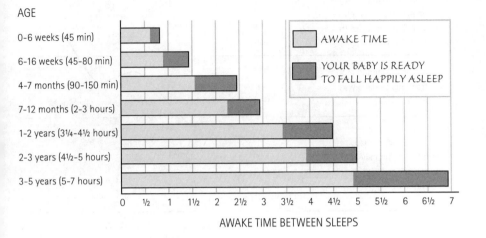

AGE

	AWAKE TIME BETWEEN SLEEPS

0-6 weeks (45 min)
6-16 weeks (45-80 min)
4-7 months (90-150 min)
7-12 months (2-3 hours)
1-2 years (3¼-4½ hours)
2-3 years (4½-5 hours)
3-5 years (5-7 hours)

AWAKE TIME

YOUR BABY IS READY
TO FALL HAPPILY ASLEEP

0   ½   1   1½   2   2½   3   3½   4   4½   5   5½   6   6½   7

AWAKE TIME BETWEEN SLEEPS

Awake times and over-stimulation

We each have an individual sensory threshold, which determines the amount of stimulation we can tolerate before we react. For instance, the obvious threshold we have is for pain. Where one woman can tolerate labour pains without any pain relief another cries out for an epidural five minutes into labour. One of the factors that affect our threshold for sensory input is how tired we are. We are best able to deal with the sound of a crying baby after a good night's sleep and tolerate a busy toddler's birthday party with greater ease if we have had an afternoon nap. Babies are even **more** sensitive to sensory input because they have an immature nervous system. When your baby is tired

- he is easily over-stimulated.
- his capacity for interactions and stimulation decreases
- he will not learn optimally from his environment.
- his frustration tolerance is low
- he will not go to sleep easily.

As your baby reaches the end of his age-appropriate awake time, he becomes drowsy and will signal that he is ready to sleep (see page 25 for signals). If you encourage sleep and put your baby to bed NOW, he should have little difficulty falling asleep unassisted. However, if you miss this timing (because you might have missed his signals), and keep him awake he will get a second wind. The second wind is brought on by flight or fight hormones released by his brain to help him cope with being over-tired. He will interact less happily during this awake time and as it draws to a close he will be more difficult to get to sleep as he is overtired. At this stage released hormones such as adrenaline (to keep him alert) and cortisol (to deal with the stress of being over-stimulated) will prevent him from falling happily asleep.

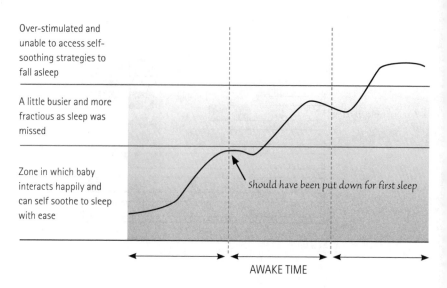

Over-stimulated and unable to access self-soothing strategies to fall asleep

A little busier and more fractious as sleep was missed

Zone in which baby interacts happily and can self soothe to sleep with ease

Should have been put down for first sleep

AWAKE TIME

If you have missed the natural dip in alertness and are battling to put your baby to sleep one of two things will happen:

- **He will require intensive strategies to fall asleep.** If he is overtired, chances are that you will have to resort to intensive strategies to settle your needy baby to sleep. Rocking him, feeding him, or even driving him in the car may be some of the desperate measures you may resort to. These sleep associations may create problems for you at night when your baby will demand the same ritual to finally fall asleep at the end of the day and again when he wakes during the night.
- **He may miss another sleep.** If all your emergency measures fail and you can't get your baby to sleep, you may find he gets a second wind (or third or fourth) and becomes busier and more irritable and fussy and even more difficult to get to sleep. He will most likely 'collapse in a heap' at the end of the day and fall into an exhausted sleep. But, because his sensory system is in such a state of over-load, he will struggle to link his sleep cycles and stay asleep for the night. This will make him more tired and grumpy the next day (because he hasn't slept properly the night before), and so the cycle continues (see below).

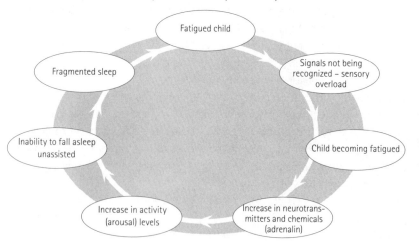

Fatigued child

Signals not being recognized – sensory overload

Fragmented sleep

Child becoming fatigued

Inability to fall asleep unassisted

Increase in activity (arousal) levels

Increase in neurotransmitters and chemicals (adrenalin)

ESTABLISHING A DAY-SLEEP ROUTINE

Now that you know how important it is for both babies and toddlers to sleep during the day, you can establish a flexible day-sleep routine for your child by using the simple guidelines below. Since every baby is different, you need to understand the principles of **when** your baby should go down and make your own routine work for your individual baby.

Watch his awake times

The first step to developing a healthy day-sleep routine regardless of age is to watch your baby's age-appropriate awake times. Take note of the time that your baby wakes in the morning or from a nap and ensure you are ready to put him back to sleep as the awake time draws to a close. See diagram on page 61 for the appropriate awake time for your baby's age.

Take note of his signals for sleep

Look out for your baby's signals that will indicate that he is starting to feel tired (see page 25). You will note that they usually occur about ten minutes before the awake time ends. These include looking away from you or a toy, rubbing his eyes and holding his ears. Sucking his hands or grizzling and fretting also indicate your baby has had enough stimulation and is ready for sleep.

Put your baby down to sleep

As soon as your baby's awake time is up, even if you are not picking up on sleep signals, take him to his sleep zone and let his sleep zone **signal sleep time**.

- Create the right sensory environment for sleep by closing the blinds or curtains and closing the door if necessary.
- Play lulling music or white noise to help him to shift into a drowsy state.
- Make sure he is warm and dry (change your baby's nappy if necessary) and hold him close to you in a sleep position.
- If applicable, encourage his sleep object.
- Swaddle your baby if he is less than three months old or still enjoys to be wrapped.
- If he is older than three months and still enjoys being swaddled to sleep, continue to do so.
- Rock him and lull him for a few minutes until he is drowsy (relaxed fists and body and drowsy eyes) then put him **down in his bed**. Remember not to dip his head, as this may wake him up

Developing a regular day routine

As each day goes by, your baby will start to develop his own sleep rhythms and routine. You will not need to force him into a **set time** for sleep each day, such as an 11 am sleep; this will only create added stress. Rather guide him into a healthy sleep routine by watching his awake times and following his lead (by acting on his signals). The times may vary slightly from day to day, but there will be a **pattern** to your day before long.

SLEEP SECRET
Sleep makes sleep.
The big message here is that all babies and toddlers need day sleeps - regular ones according to their age. Do not be tempted to keep your baby awake during the day to improve his sleep at night.

SLEEP SECRET
Holding your baby close to you and rocking him will help to shift him into a drowsy state to prepare him for sleep. The trick is to put him into his bed in this drowsy state, not asleep, so that he can put himself to sleep.

There are some babies who appear to cope well on very little sleep and prolonged periods of awake time. If your baby is thriving and happy and does **not** resist sleep during the day and at bedtime, and **sleeps well** at night, count yourself lucky that you have such a contented child. You will, obviously, not need to change anything in terms of your baby's routine if this is the case.

For age appropriate suggested daytime routines read the chapter relevant for your baby's age.

WHEN DAY ROUTINES DON'T WORK OUT

Nothing is more frustrating than battling to get your baby down when you know that your baby is tired and needs to sleep. You are reading his signals, preventing over-stimulation, but are still struggling to establish a regular day sleep routine. Sometimes circumstances make it difficult to get day routines right. Most of these situations are temporary, and if handled correctly, pass without too much fuss. Let's discuss them and equip you with strategies to help you get it right.

Young babies

On the day of your baby's birth he will have a period of calm-alert wakefulness, which is a wonderful time for initial bonding to take place. Thereafter, most babies sleep a lot in the early days, waking to feed sleepily before falling asleep again. However, at around two weeks of age, the 'honeymoon' period ends and your once sleepy and calm baby wakes up! As much as your baby needs sleep, he may fuss a lot and begin to resist sleep or wake after very short periods of sleep. Don't be fooled into thinking that because he is so alert, he does not need to sleep. Follow these steps to help your young baby fall asleep:

- After **45 minutes** of awake time, (which is literally enough time to complete a feed, nappy change and a cuddle) wrap him up snugly in a swaddle blanket and take him into his sleep zone.
- Play soft music, or white noise in the background.
- Keep him swaddled most of the time at this age, especially when he is sleeping.
- Rock him gently until he is really drowsy and put him into his bed. If he begins to fuss and squirm, turn him onto his side facing away from you and put one hand on his shoulder and with the other hand, hold or pat him. Say 'ssshhh' in a gentle voice, and keep your hands in this position until he stops squirming and drops off to sleep. **Note this is not letting him cry**, it is just giving him calming, deep pressure to help him fall asleep.
- He should be sleeping on his side or on his back at this age.
- If he fusses, and won't settle after a few minutes, pick him up *gently* and rock him until he is calm again.
- Try to stay in the sleep zone while you get him calm and drowsy, and try again.
- If he remains unsettled after about 15 minutes, do not lose sight of your goal

to get him to **sleep** and use strategies to get him to sleep no matter what you have to do to achieve this. Try placing him in a sling or pram and walk with him, or let him suck on your finger or a dummy until he falls asleep.

- Don't worry about spoiling your baby, or creating bad habits at this young age. Young babies do not have memory that will allow them to form habits until at least four months of age.
- At this tender age, many babies need a little help in the form of sensory input to help them settle. Mimic the world of the womb (a very calming sensory environment) through
  - movement – moving or rocking
  - sounds – white noise, shshshing or humming
  - touch – deep pressure in the form of a swaddle blanket and/or a sling, which makes him feel secure.

Cusp ages

The suggested length of babies' awake times have been tried and tested and work for almost all babies. Be guided by your baby's awake times as opposed to a rigid schedule, and you will find your baby will settle easily into sleep. However, at certain times in your baby or toddler's life, he may begin to protest about going to sleep during the day. This often happens because he is on the **cusp** of being able to do without a certain sleep. At these times, the length of the awake time in the afternoon simply has to be stretched to accommodate bedtime, which will then be adjusted to an earlier time.

These tricky stages are age appropriate. Called **cusp ages**, they occur around the following stages:

NINE TO 12 MONTHS

Between six and nine months, most babies are having two to three short naps and one longer sleep (depending on the length of their sleeps). Between nine months and a year, the late afternoon nap may need to drop away or be shortened if it interferes with your baby settling in the evening. Some babies still need to have a short 'power nap' to see them through the evening rituals of bathing, feeding etc. Be sure to wake your baby by 4:30 pm if he is having an afternoon nap so that bedtime can be kept between 6 and 7 pm. Towards the end of this stage, this nap will fall away and there will be a longer stretch in the afternoon. When this happens, bring bedtime earlier for a few weeks to help your baby to adjust.

FIFTEEN TO 24 MONTHS

Most one-year-old babies are still having two sleeps a day. But it won't be long before your baby starts to resist the afternoon sleep (especially if he catches a whiff of activity in the air!) and have one longer sleep instead of two. Keep taking your baby to his sleep zone so that he can sleep if he wants to. Even if he doesn't sleep for long, or simply has some quiet time in his cot, it is better than no sleep at all.

This can be a tricky time because he can't really manage with being awake for so long, but won't settle easily for two sleeps a day.

To adjust at this cusp age, drop the morning sleep and bring the afternoon sleep to late morning then move your entire bedtime routine earlier, so that he is asleep by 6 pm. Don't worry about this resulting in an early morning – research has shown that early bedtimes promote healthier sleep at night and do not result in early rising.

TWO-AND-A-HALF TO FIVE YEARS

Depending on your baby, he will drop his day sleep altogether at some stage. When this happens, chances are that he is not ready to go through the day with no sleep, but has started to resist the day sleep or going to bed in the evening. Keep encouraging the healthy sleep habit of an afternoon rest-time after lunch, but accept that if he does not fall asleep within the hour, he has just had a rest and has dropped the day sleep for that day.

When your baby is going through a cusp stage, you may find that he needs a catch-up day sleep every couple of days, but will be perfectly fine with a bit of quiet time on the days he does not sleep.

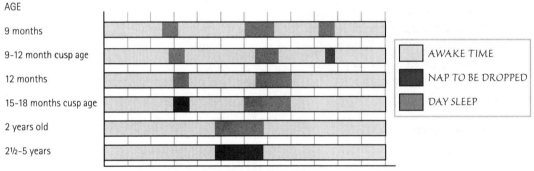

AGE

9 months

9-12 month cusp age

12 months

15-18 months cusp age

2 years old

2½-5 years

AWAKE TIME

NAP TO BE DROPPED

DAY SLEEP

NUMBER OF DAY SLEEPS

Day care and day-sleep routines

When you are looking for suitable day care for your baby outside of your home, it is important to check that they allocate reasonable, age-appropriate sleep times for all their charges. The fact that all the babies go to sleep at the same time means that your baby will probably fit in well with what all the other babies are doing and develop a good day sleep routine.

However, if you have a particularly fussy or sensitive baby, it might be necessary to make special arrangements so that the staff can accommodate your baby's particular routine. No facility should refuse you this right, so if you come up against resistance, you might want to consider moving your baby to one that will accommodate you.

Try to be consistent by keeping your weekend routine the same as his day care during the week.

Out and about for day-sleep routines

Most babies fall asleep very easily while travelling in the car. If your baby falls asleep while you travel, try to leave him to sleep for at least one sleep cycle (45 min) once you arrive at your destination. Try to have your baby go to sleep in his cot for at least one sleep a day and **always** for evening bedtime. In this way bad habits of falling asleep in the car will be avoided. (See page 135 for tips to break this habit if it is a problem for you.)

Older babies and toddlers tend to sleep at a more specific time of day. If your toddler has to fit in with your plans for a period of time or on a certain day, try to make sure he travels before or after sleep times. For instance if you fetch your older child from school at 1 pm, try to make sure your toddler has an allocated time for sleep at 11 am so that he has had two hours sleep and preferably wakes naturally before you collect his older sibling.

Changing time zones

When changing time zones it is easier to use the awake-time principles than a prescribed sleep schedule. From the time you land in the new time zone, watch the awake times, as you would have anyway during the day. If your baby is not over-tired, he will adjust to the new time zone with ease. In the evening, use the sleep zone and your bedtime routine to effectively signal to your baby that it is night time. (See Chapter 7 for bedtime routine.)

Another useful method to use when changing time zones for a long period of time (more than two weeks) is to start from a week before, to slowly ease your baby into the **new** time zone, by either waking him up slightly earlier each morning, or by stretching his bedtime by 30 minutes or so each day. Whether you *wake earlier* or *stretch later* will depend on what time zone you are moving into. Before returning home, begin a week before you leave by doing the same thing. Expect things to be a bit higgledy-piggledy for a while when you get home (especially if **you** are jet-lagged), but know that it will pass and your baby will settle back into his old routine.

WAKING YOUR BABY FROM SLEEP

Day sleep is critically linked to night sleep and literally the more your baby sleeps during the day, the more he will sleep at night. There are only four reasons that babies should be woken from day sleeps:

- If your newborn is reversing day and night, wake him to feed four hourly.
- If your baby is not gaining weight or is ill and you have been advised by your doctor or baby nurse to wake him for nutrition or medication.
- If your toddler sleeps late in the afternoon and resists bedtime, shorten this afternoon sleep.
- If your child (older than two years) is waking extremely early in the morning (before 5 am), it is worth trying to limit his day sleep to one hour. Be prepared for some miserable afternoons, and if you see no improvement after a few days, stop waking him.

▪ SUMMARY OF ESTABLISHING A HEALTHY DAY-SLEEP ROUTINE

- Your baby's age-appropriate **awake times** are the length of time your baby can be happily awake before becoming over stimulated.
- If you watch your baby's awake time, are in tune with his **sleep signals** and put him down to sleep in his bed when he is ready, he will fall asleep easily.
- **Day-sleep routines** are important and develop over time.
- At certain **cusp ages** your baby's day-sleep routine will change.
- Remember, **day sleep begets night sleep** but there may be exceptional times when you have to wake your baby from sleep.

STEPS TO A GOOD NIGHT'S SLEEP

1. You have realistic expectations of your baby's sleep.
2. You have introduced sensory calming activities.
3. Your baby has a consistent and calming zone for sleep.
4. You have ruled out hunger and nutritional needs as a cause of night wakings.
5. You are certain no medical issues are causing night wakings.
6. You have established a good day-sleep routine.

Sleep associations

CHAPTER 7

STEP 7: PRIME YOUR BABY FOR INDEPENDENT SELF-SOOTHING AT NIGHT USING HEALTHY SLEEP ASSOCIATIONS

Andrea longed for just one evening when she and her husband could sit down together for dinner without any interruption. Each night as she put ten-month-old Emma to sleep she would have to enact a ritual that tied her to her baby. Emma would only go to sleep if Andrea held her and she could stroke Andrea's hair. This was endearing when she was tiny and would drop off quite easily but nowadays Andrea could be there for up to an hour while Emma stroked her hair. But worse was Emma's latest antic of crying for Andrea in the middle of the night in order to fall back to sleep stroking Andrea's hair. It was getting so ridiculous that Andrea had thought about cutting off a strand for Emma to use on her own!

When we go to bed each night, we all have certain sleep rituals that help us switch off to prepare for sleep. For most people, sleep associations or rituals entail sensory calming strategies that prime them for sleep. We might have a warm bath or drink before turning off the light, turning over, tucking the duvet just right and falling asleep. When we rouse in the middle of the night (as we move between sleep cycles), chances are that we will re-enact some of the ritual, such as getting back into our favourite position, plumping our pillow or putting our hand near our face. Most of this is done completely subconsciously but it is nevertheless a sleep association we use to help us go back to sleep.

PROBLEM ASSOCIATIONS

Sleep associations may be the cause of your child's sleep problems if
- she is over four months of age
- she always needs you to provide specific sensory calming strategies for her to fall asleep
- she always falls asleep in your arms, whilst feeding, in the car, etc.
- she wakes regularly at night and will not re-settle unless the sleep association is re-enacted.

As the word suggests, sleep associations are specific sensory experiences your baby **associates with sleep** and uses to fall asleep or stay asleep. There are two types of sleep associations:

- those that prime us for sleep and calm us **before** sleep, such as a warm bath, and
- those that help us actually **fall asleep**, such as a sleep position.

For your baby, the sleep association that *primes her* for sleep is a **bedtime routine** (dealt with later in this chapter – see page 73). Sleep associations babies use to *actually fall asleep* are called **sleep soothers**.

SLEEP SOOTHERS

As we learnt in Chapter I, if your baby is healthy and not hungry, your goal is not so much to have her sleep through the night, but to have her go back to sleep on her own when she stirs or wakes between sleep cycles. The way in which she does this is to self-soothe using specific sensory input independently.

Choosing appropriate sleep soothers

Some of the soothers your baby uses independently are on her own body, such as her thumb, her voice and her hair. Other soothers you should introduce to your baby are a sleep soother such as a security blanket, a favourite soft toy or a dummy.

Try to find something your baby can use independently rather than something she for which she will depend on you to provide for her in the middle of the night.

Sensory component	Dependent on you	Independent soothers
Touch	Stroking your hair Being patted to sleep	Stroking a piece of satin or silk or fleece or a soft toy Touching her own face Stroking her own hair
Movement	Car Pram Rocking to sleep	Rocking her head Moving her hands Kicking her legs
Sucking	Your breast Your finger Feeding bottle Dummy (until she learns to use it independently)	Thumb Dummy (becomes an independent soother)
Body position	In your arms Being held in a certain favourite position	Wedging herself against the top of the cot Sleeping on a specific side
Sounds	Mom singing	Humming Singing or moaning to herself White noise CD or machine or fountain

SUCKING

Non-nutritive sucking (in other words, sucking whilst **not** feeding) really helps to calm young babies. Some babies learn to suck on their own hands from a very early age; others prefer to suck a dummy. Both are excellent soothers for young babies. Do not stop your baby from sucking (remember it does not mean he is teething or hungry if he puts his hands in his mouth – he may simply be needing to calm down a bit) but guide your baby into a method you prefer.

THUMB SUCKING

Thumb sucking is an excellent self-calming strategy and is the first very clever, independent skill your baby learns. Your life will be easier if your baby can calm herself in this manner, especially at sleep time.

The advantages of thumb or hand sucking is that it is something your baby can use independently from very early on. The disadvantage is that thumb suckers may have a higher risk of needing orthodontic treatment at a later age. Whether thumb sucking will result in bucked teeth depends on your family's predisposition and how long your child sucks her thumb. It is harder to get rid of a thumb-sucking habit as you can't conveniently 'lose' a thumb (like you can a dummy) but if your baby is fussy, and sucking on her thumb really helps her to calm, worry about that later. Remember, the issue is to get your baby to calm, so that sleep can follow.

In the early days, the startle and moro reflexes move the arms outwards when young babies are distressed, making it very hard to self-calm while crying. Help your baby find her hands to suck on to self-calm, by swaddling her hands close to her face. Often this won't be enough to sufficiently calm her and a dummy can also be used.

DUMMIES

On a sensory level, your baby needs to suck in order to be calm, and if she is not doing it herself (by sucking her hands or thumb) a dummy is a very effective tool. Getting rid of the dummy is a bridge you can cross later. It will depend on your baby – some just reject the dummy naturally in the first year, others need to be rewarded for giving it up in the toddler years.

Teaching your baby to use a dummy independently

Until your baby is about seven months of age, she will not be able to use her dummy independently. If her dummy has fallen out of her mouth while she is sleeping, she may well need to suck on it again in order to settle as she moves between sleep cycles. Many babies begin to wake up during the night needing to suck on their dummies for comfort owing to the discomfort of teething (between six and nine months of age). Accept that 'dummy patrol' is something you may have to do for a period of time to get your baby to fall back asleep quickly and easily, but take comfort in knowing that from about seven to eight months of age, you can begin to teach your baby to use her dummy independently, especially at night

If your baby is waking you to put in the dummy at night, there are four steps to help her (if she is older than seven months) use her dummy independently at night:

- In the first few days, keep putting her dummy into her mouth when she cries at night, but during the day never put the dummy directly into her mouth. Rather place the dummy in her hand so that she learns to put it in her mouth herself in daylight hours.
- Attach her dummy onto a dummy ribbon or dummy chain during waking hours, so that is available for her if she needs it. When she needs her dummy, guide her hand onto the ribbon or chain until she finds the dummy. With time, she will learn to pop it in herself in daylight hours.
- Once she has achieved daytime dummy independence, do the same at night – never place it in her mouth, but rather put the dummy in her hand or attach it to a sleep blanky and put that in her hand so she must do the final step of putting the dummy in her mouth on her own.
- When she has advanced to that stage (usually within a few days if she is older than eight months), stop placing the dummy in her hand and guide her hand to the dummy in the dark. The next night put every dummy in the house in her cot giving her the best possible odds of finding one in the dark!

Be prepared for a few nights of disturbed sleep until you get this right – but persevere, it's worth it!

Teaching your baby to use a sleep soother

A security blanky or sleep soother is the best sleep association your baby can have and something that most babies take to quite easily. When your baby is very young, a sleep soother is not necessary, as **you** will be doing the soothing, but when she is about three months of age, choose something that you know your baby might like. Choose something soft, small enough to put into a nappy bag and not be a suffocation risk and, most importantly, something you can replace if your toddler loses her beloved security blanket a year down the line. Examples of good comfort objects are a small soft-toy, a small fleece blanket, a burp cloth or a small blanket with satin borders or tags.

To introduce a security object, give it to her whenever she fusses. Whether she is distressed by pain, irritation or tiredness during the day, give her a hug, comfort her **and** tuck the object into her body. Put it on your shoulder if it's a blanky and let her cuddle into both the blanky and you. After a week or two of consistently offering the sleep object **with** your comfort, your baby will start to associate the object with your comfort – which is another reason it is called an association object.

BEDTIME ROUTINE

It was New Year's Eve 1999 and Lynne's friends had decided to go away to some chalets near town to see in the new Millennium. Owing to the shortage of baby sitters that night, all four babies who were between the ages of nine and 16 months would be baby-sat in the same room. Lynne was concerned that Josh would be too excited to fall asleep with his camp cot wedged between three others. However, Lynne implemented the exact bedtime routine as she did every other night. After a bath and a quiet story, she gave Josh his final bottle in her arms and put him down amongst the yells and chattering of the other babies and walked out. Fifteen minutes later, she returned to find Josh in dreamland.

The value of a consistent bedtime routine cannot be underestimated and it is probably one of the key sleep associations you can use with your baby. A bedtime routine is so important, because it acts as a signal to the brain to begin to shift down from a calm alert (and wakeful) state to the all-important drowsy state before sleep can happen.

Most parents have made the mistake of expecting their baby to fall asleep easily and quickly after an exciting and stimulating awake time. We know now that this is most unlikely to happen. The concept of a bedtime routine is to use calming sensory input to settle your baby to a drowsy state so that she will be able to self-sooth to sleep thereafter.

SENSORY SOOTHING TOOLS TO USE WITH YOUR BEDTIME ROUTINE

Sensory component	Bedtime routine ideas
Touch	• Warm bath • Soft, warm towel • Soft, warm clothes • Soothing massage
Movement	• Rocking your baby gently in your arms • Pushing your baby in a pram to enhance drowsiness • Walking with your baby in a pouch or sling
Sucking	• Dummy • Thumb • Breast or bottle feeding
Body position	• Comfortable position in care-giver's arms
Visual	• Dark/dimmed room • Night light for toddlers • Read or show a bedtime story
Smells	• Lavender • Chamomile • Vanilla • Familiar smell of sleep blanky
Sounds	• White noise • Lullaby • Classical music

Suggested bedtime routine

Predetermine a bedtime appropriate for your child's age – between 6 and 7 pm is usually best depending on afternoon naps. Bear in mind that this time may be flexible, but keep the same actual routine as far as possible.

- Bath your baby about an hour before bedtime and put soothing scented bathtime products such as lavender oil, chamomile etc into your child's bath. Sit with your child while she plays in the bath remembering to keep it relatively calm and quiet. Wrap her in a warm towel when you take her out of the bath.
- Go directly to the sleep zone (which you have prepared to be the ideal sensory environment with a dimmed light etc. – see page 38). Do not take your baby out of this sleep zone until the next morning.
- Play soft soothing lullabies or sing to her.
- Massage her with soothing, suitably fragrant bedtime products, such as lavender massage oil or chamomile cream.
- Dress her in soft night clothes and use a good quality night-time nappy.
- Play quiet games or read to her during 'floor time' before bed.
- Read a predetermined number of books to her. For ideas of good bedtime books, see appendix D (page 168).
- Turn off or dim the light and offer your child her sleep soother at this point.
- Give her the last breast or bottle feed of the evening in the dark room in your arms. If your child is sleeping in a bed, rather sit on a chair for this last feed.
- If feeding has not made her drowsy enough, you may have to stand and rock her, or sing her a lullaby to help her get drowsy.
- When she is drowsy **but not asleep**, put her into her bed (remember not head first!), tuck her sleep object into her body, say goodnight quietly, and leave the room.

By keeping your baby's bedtime routine as consistent as possible, it will become a very important *sleep cue* that will really ease your baby to sleep. A consistent bedtime routine is important especially if your day has been busy or your baby's sleep space changes, for instance when you are on holiday.

UNDESIRABLE SLEEP ASSOCIATIONS

Be sure that your baby's sleep associations can be used independently. It is easy to fall into the trap of using any tool to settle your baby. By far the most common sleep trap is feeding to sleep. Allowing your baby to fall asleep while feeding not only encourages undesirable sleep associations, but can also contribute towards recurrent ear infections and teeth decay.

In toddlers, boundary issues and strong wills often result in habits that are difficult to break. By not teaching your toddler to fall asleep independently of you, for instance if you still have to lie with her while she strokes your hair, she may not have confidence to tackle other independent tasks, such as separating from you to go to playschool.

How do you know when you are ready to address undesirable sleep associations? Well, it is a combination of being exhausted, frustrated and prepared to do something about them. Keep reading the next chapters of this book to learn age-appropriate strategies to help you on your journey.

SUMMARY OF SLEEP ASSOCIATIONS FOR HEALTHY SLEEP HABITS

- Your baby needs a **sleep soother** that she can use independently to support healthy sleep.
- Encourage a sleep soother from an **early age**.
- Good sleep soothers have **sensory calming** qualities.
- You should teach your baby to use a sleep soother such as a blanky or dummy **independently** from seven months of age
- A **calming bedtime routine** is essential is setting the stage for sleep
- Follow your **bedtime routine consistently** while establishing good sleep habits. This becomes a pattern you can use wherever you are to get your baby to sleep.

STEPS TO A GOOD NIGHT'S SLEEP
1. You have realistic expectations of your baby's sleep.
2. You have introduced sensory calming activities.
3. Your baby has a consistent and calming zone for sleep.
4. You have ruled out hunger and nutritional needs as a cause of night wakings.
5. You are certain no medical issues are causing night wakings.
6. You have established a good day-sleep routine.
7. You have helped your baby establish healthy, independent sleep associations.

CHAPTER 8

Separation issues

STEP 8: DEAL WITH SEPARATION ISSUES AS THEY ARISE

Maria hates leaving Joshua every day. She has been back at work for a month now, having been lucky enough to stay at home for the first seven months of Josh's life. Josh was sleeping well but as luck would have it, when Maria started work, Josh started waking up at night. Now he frequently wakes three times at night and Maria is falling apart with fatigue during the day. When Josh wakes during the night, Maria simply has to resettle him with a pat or a cuddle and he goes back to sleep quickly. Maria is wondering whether her returning to work has resulted in these night-time disruptions.

Sleep is the very first separation between you and your baby. This separation may create anxiety for many parents in the early days. For this reason, you may have chosen to have your baby in your room for the first few weeks, as hearing your little one's fluttery breaths and new-baby grunts reassured you that your baby was okay.

It is understandable that at some stage in the first few years, your baby or toddler, too, will suffer some anxiety when separating from the person he depends on so completely, his parent.

While separation anxiety is present for parents from the day their baby is born, babies only seem to experience it from about six months of age.

SEPARATION ANXIETY

Separation anxiety may be the cause of your baby's sleep problems if
- He is older than seven months
- He is easily comforted by your presence at night
- He is dealing with a significant change in his life
- He has been hospitalized or has recently been ill
- He has always been more sensitive to sensory input
- You battle significantly with being separated from him
- You have suffered a significant loss in your life such as the loss of your mother or a child.

HOW SEPARATION ANXIETY DEVELOPS

By the end of your baby's first day of life, he recognizes your face. Experiments have shown that when day-old babies are shown pictures of their mother's face, they suck harder on a dummy, indicating obvious preference for their mother's face.

Although your baby recognizes you when he sees you from early on and will soon be excited to see you; if his needs for love, cuddles and nutrition are attended to, he does not miss you for two reasons. Firstly, he has no memory of you when you are not around because the part of the brain that contributes to memory only develops later in the first year. Secondly, the young baby has no concept of time and space, so whether you are gone for a second or a few hours, the separation is equal for your newborn.

All this blissful ignorance disappears when your baby develops **object permanence**, at around seven months of age. Object permanence is the realization that something exists even if you can't see it. At five months old, when a toy drops from your baby's line of vision, he won't pursue it or look for it as it literally ceases to exist in his little mind. However, usually by eight months, your baby will start to look for something when it drops or moves out of his line of vision. At this point, he has worked out that the object exists even if he's not holding it – a reflection that he has developed object permanence.

As this realization dawns and memory develops, your baby will likewise begin to realize that when *you* leave him, you still exist. It does not please him to be separated from you as he has by now formed a strong attachment to you and this separation may cause him to cry when you leave him.

SLEEP SECRET
By comforting your baby with your **voice**, he will learn that even if he can't see you, you are still around. If he becomes used to being comforted by your voice, you can use your voice effectively in the middle of the night, by simply calling out 'I can hear you, I love you, go back to sleep!' when he wakes up.

THE EFFECT OF SEPARATION ANXIETY ON SLEEP

Separation anxiety is a common and completely normal part of your baby's development. The downside is that it may have a negative effect on your baby's sleep. Between seven and ten months of age, your baby may protest as you put him down to sleep and leave the room. He may also wake at night to call you back to be sure that you still exist. There are four main types of separation anxiety that affect sleep:

• Age appropriate separation anxiety
• Separation anxiety related to a life change
• Separation anxiety related to sensory processing problems
• Maternal separation anxiety.

In order to effectively manage sleep problems, you need to identify which type of separation issue is affecting your baby's sleep. From there you can go on to deal with issues around separation in an appropriate manner.

NORMAL AGE-APPROPRIATE SEPARATION ANXIETY

Normal separation anxiety affects most babies after seven months of age and again in the toddler years and will naturally resolve as your baby gets older. To deal with sleep problems related to age-appropriate separation anxiety, you need to help your **baby feel secure** with separations. It is important to be consistent, so that he will become secure with the fact that you *are* around, and that you *will* return.

Play separation games

To encourage your baby to develop object permanence and show him that separations are met with cheerful reunions, play games with him.

Peek-a-boo. Put a face cloth over your face or in front of your baby's face briefly and say 'Peek-a-boo!' as you drop the fabric to reveal yourself to him. Young babies love this game and it helps them realize that you still exist when they can't see you.

Find the toy. Place any interesting or loved object such as a dummy or teddy under a blanket or sheet and say 'Where's teddy?' then pull the fabric back revealing the item. You will know that your baby is getting the idea of object permanence when he lifts the fabric himself to find the object.

Hide and seek. Hide around the corner of the couch or bed and call your baby. If he looks towards the sound of your voice or crawls towards you, respond by showing yourself with a big smile and laugh. This teaches your baby that you still exist when he can't see you and a happy reunion accompanies this brief separation.

Handle separations positively

When you separate from your baby, you may well have feelings of anxiety, sadness or guilt but it is vital that you do not communicate this to your baby. Remember that separations from your baby are important for you, whether it is to go to work or to have a few hours of quality time for yourself when going to gym or shopping. If the message you give your baby is positive and confident he is less likely to consider the separation negatively or with anxiety.

Do not be tempted to sneak out and disappear to avoid the tears. Try to handle separations matter-of-factly and **always say goodbye**. This is very important so that your baby will trust that you will always let him know when you are leaving for any period of time. Even if your baby turns on the tears and clutches to you as you leave, be positive and leave after a happy goodbye. Be assured that your baby will settle minutes after you leave.

Make a little photograph album of pictures of you saying goodbye and pictures of you returning and show them to your baby.

Happy reunions

Just as you need to be consistent with your goodbyes, you must always return with a happy greeting and spend time reuniting with your baby. You may find that your baby is a little clingy after you return – don't worry, this is normal. If you expect this and put aside a bit of time to re connect, your baby will manage better the next time you separate.

Establish attachment to a security object

Take the time to help your baby attach to a security object such as a blanky or soft toy. One of the goals of parenting is that your baby will move from complete dependence on you to independence. This is a process that takes time and for a long time your baby will be fully dependent on you for comfort. The concept of a transition or security object is that your baby will begin to shift his unwavering attachment to you to an interim security object. By achieving this, he is well on his way to becoming more independent as he grows and develops into a preschooler.

To help your baby attach to a security object choose one only and offer it to him from the age of about three months, along with your comfort, whenever he cries. If your baby is tired or over stimulated or has hurt himself, place the blanky or soft toy on your shoulder so that as your baby cuddles in to you, he receives comfort from the object too.

By six months of age, your baby will begin to associate comfort with this security object. If he is older than six months, nutritionally sound and healthy, he should not need to call for you to comfort him to sleep when he wakes at night. By attaching to a security blanky or sleep soother, he is less likely to wake you when he goes through periods of night wakings related to comfort seeking. It is always a good idea to make sure it is well within his reach during the night, so try to get into the habit of checking for that before you go to bed.

SEPARATION ANXIETY RELATED TO A LIFE CHANGE

Life's circumstances may bring times when an otherwise easy baby becomes very clingy and suddenly develops anxiety with every separation from his main care-giver. In this case other causes of separation anxiety must be considered. The following are common causes of separation anxiety:

- Mother returning to work
- Moving house
- Birth of a sibling
- Death of a grandparent
- Starting crèche or preschool
- Marital discord or divorce
- Hospitalizations and illness
- Change of nanny or caregiver.

During these periods, make allowances for your baby feeling disrupted by spending more quality time with him during the day.

Watch Wait & Wonder

Spending one-on-one quality time with your baby is the purpose of this technique. Designed by psychotherapist Elizabeth Muir and modified by Dr Michael Zilibowitz, Developmental and Behavioural Paediatrician, *Watch Wait &*

Wonder has been proven to decrease separation anxiety and will enhance your relationship with your child.

To follow the WWW programme, schedule 30 minutes three times a week of totally undisturbed time with your baby or toddler. Turn off the phone, do not attend to other matters, and simply focus on being with your child.

1. *Watch him play.* Do so uncritically, without intervening just watching him and following his lead as he plays. Do not teach or interfere at all. Use age-appropriate toys and sit on the floor with him.
2. *Wait for your baby to include you.* Sometimes this may mean spending the time just watching, but often you will find your baby will happily include you in one of his tasks. Once he initiates interaction with you, play on his level, not directing what he is doing.
3. *Wonder about what your baby's play means to him.* This will help you connect with your baby resulting in him feeling more secure.

Choose child care options wisely

One of the greatest concerns when we have when we leave our baby in someone else's care, is whether they will be able to meet his physical and emotional needs. In order for you to be able to say goodbye positively and feel okay with separations you must choose your child care carefully. Follow these guidelines when choosing a caregiver:

- Try not to place your baby into care where there is a ratio of more than four babies to one caregiver, until the age of three years.
- Ensure there is consistency of care for your child, in other words not a group of three carers for 12 children. Although the ratio of carers to children is correct, the carer may change from day to day and task to task.
- If your child is younger than three years, try to find care that consists of a small group of children (such as a day mother, or a dedicated nanny), rather than a large care centre.

SEPARATION ANXIETY IN A SENSITIVE BABY

Although Joshua is waking at night due to separation issues, he is not nearly as bad as his cousin Matt. At 19 months, Matt is known by all and sundry as a 'Velcro baby'. He clings to his mother's skirt at every social function, cries whenever she leaves the room and will not even be left with his dad or granny. His dad thinks that he is being over-protected by his mom and has suggested that Matt needs to be 'toughened up'. Matt's sleep has always been bad and his mom is being worn down by fatigue and being constantly clung to.

Sensory causes of separation anxiety

For a laid-back baby, a separation from Mom may not create too much anxiety. However, for babies like Matt any separation from Mom may be an issue. This difference has to do with the individual baby's temperament, specifically the way he processes sensory information.

We all have a specific threshold for sensory information, just as we have a pain threshold. If your baby's threshold is high, he will be able to deal with a lot of sensory input and be happy and interactive without becoming over-stimulated. However, if your baby's threshold is low, he will have a very low tolerance for sensory input. Even soft and gentle touch may then seem threatening and painful. If all touch is threatening, being bumped by another toddler or even stroked kindly by granny may not be pleasurable. Likewise, if your baby has a low tolerance for sounds and smells, a birthday party may become an intolerable event owing to the unpredictability of the sensory input.

For these babies, Mom is considered 'safe space' as she is **predictable** on a sensory level. A sensitive baby's mother knows just how to touch and speak to her child and understands the amount of warning her child needs before he is exposed to a sensory event. The sensitive child has difficulty separating from this person who keeps his world predictable, and is understandably anxious when this happens. Being stuck to mom makes the world more predictable and less threatening. If this is your child, you will now understand why separation from you creates such heightened levels of anxiety for him.

Managing separation anxiety due to sensory issues

Dealing with a clingy baby or toddler who never separates from her during the day and in addition to that wakes at night is exhausting for any mother. The following strategies will help you manage your baby's separation issues:

- The underlying sensory issues will need to be addressed by an occupational therapist specializing in sensory integration. The OT will help you structure your baby's day so that he is less sensitive to sensory input.
- Keep play dates short and choose your baby's playmates carefully so that separations from you, even to play a few feet away, are unthreatening. In this way your child will gain confidence with separations.
- Your child's sleep is poor not only because of fear of separation but owing to the underlying sensory processing issues. See Appendix A (page 159) for information on sensory processing issues affecting sleep.

COPING WITH MATERNAL SEPARATION ANXIETY

Tanya had lost her mother when she was nine, her stepmother when she was fifteen, and then she suffered a miscarriage at seven months into her last pregnancy. When she carried her next baby to full term, she was delighted by little Kate and thoroughly enjoyed being a mother, but whenever Kate was out of her sight, even if she was with her Dad, Tanya began to suffer the symptoms of a panic attack. At night she found herself leaning over Kate's cot repeatedly and would pick Kate up to feed her at the slightest sign of waking.

Most mothers suffer a degree of anxiety when they separate from their little ones but for the majority this anxiety does pass and does not affect their ability to separate from their baby at sleep times. Occasionally a mother may find herself unreasonably consumed by anxiety at the smallest separation from her baby. When she must **leave** her baby to sleep or to go to work or even for personal time, such a mom is overwhelmed by fear, guilt and sadness.

If you recognize these emotions in yourself, your separation anxiety is probably affecting your baby's sleep. You may be reacting too quickly to your baby when he sleeps, responding when he just grunts or cries out as he turns over. You may find yourself wishing for your baby to wake so that you can be sure he is okay. In its extreme you may find yourself touching or rousing your baby even when he is sleeping peacefully.

Why this unusual degree of maternal separation anxiety occurs is often unclear but the following are predisposing factors that you should be alerted to:
- A poor relationship with your own mother.
- Loss of your mother or significant other at a young age, resulting in fears of abandonment or loss.
- Loss of a baby through still birth, multiple miscarriages or cot death.
- A poor relationship with your husband.
- A very colicky baby may elicit these feelings as you have concerns over how anyone else would cope with your baby if you are not around.
- First time mothers are also more susceptible to maternal separation anxiety.

If you find yourself experiencing unnaturally severe concerns over separation, this may have an effect on your baby's sleep because you may unwittingly rouse him when he is sleeping to allay the fear you have of losing him or being separated from him. On a subconscious level you are experiencing the separation of sleep as a trauma. To cope with maternal separation anxiety
- you need to come to terms with the fact that separations from your baby are normal and healthy, and
- you may need to see a psychologist to deal with any unresolved losses you may have experienced and to develop coping strategies for separations.

DEALING WITH SEPARATION ANXIETY AT NIGHT

Separation anxiety affects sleep in different ways at different ages:

Six to 12 months

As already mentioned, once your baby establishes object permanence, separation anxiety at night may affect his sleep. During this period, your baby may wake during light sleep states needing to be reassured by you.

Follow these simple guidelines to help him through this normal developmental phase.

- When he cries out in the night, respond to him immediately by telling him quietly and gently: 'Go to sleep my angel, ssshhhh …' comfort him with a sleep soother or a favourite soft toy, and leave the room. You do not want to feed or rock him back to sleep, as this may start a bad habit, but you do need to respond to him to demonstrate to him that you do return to him after a separation.
- During the day always say goodbye when you leave him, even when you leave the room to have a shower and always greet him happily on your return, so that he learns that separations are accompanied by happy reunions.
- A sleep soother is vital at this stage so that your baby transfers his need for comfort from you to an object which he can use independently when he wakes at night.
- Finally, manage this stage with lots of hugs and cuddles and bear with it – as with most challenges in the first year, this too will pass.

Eighteen months to preschooler

During this period, your toddler may become anxious at bedtime, and may call out to you frequently during the night, or come through to your room due to fears of being alone. This stage emerges after 18 months, when your toddler has developed imagination and begins to suffer from nightmares and imagined 'bogymen'.

Every toddler is different and the degree to which yours will be affected may vary substantially from other children you know.

- Have a night light on in his room or passage or bathroom, so that he is not in the dark should he wake.
- Limit television completely for at least two to three hours before bed as this has been linked to fears and increased nightmares.
- If your toddler won't stay in bed you may have to put firm boundaries in place to encourage him to stay in bed, such as sitting with him until he is asleep **if** he stays in bed and weaning this down to returning every five minutes until he is asleep **if** he stays in bed. (More about this in Chapter 15.)
- Play a radio or white noise CD softly in the room for background noise
- If desperate, let him sleep on a little mattress on the floor next to your bed, should he wake frequently from nightmares during the night. (More about this later in Chapter 15)

Remember, separation anxiety is real and must be dealt with by responding to your baby or toddler with empathy and care – it will pass in time. But while it lasts, to avoid long-term bad habits developing, be firm about not falling into the trap of feeding, rocking or co-sleeping if these are habits you do not wish to encourage.

SUMMARY OF SEPARATION ANXIETY

- Separation anxiety is a **normal developmental phase** that may affect sleep.
- It typically affects babies aged **between six and ten months** and again in the toddler years.
- Use strategies to **normalize separations** for your baby by playing games during the day.
- At night **comfort** your baby and use a night light for your toddler.
- Separation anxiety may be **exacerbated** by a life change, if your baby has a low sensory threshold or if you have issues with separating from your baby.
- You may be experiencing **maternal separation anxiety** which affects your ability to separate from your baby in a healthy manner to allow him to sleep.
- Remember, this phase **will pass** and try not to use strategies to get your baby back to sleep that will make him more dependent on you at night (such as feeding or rocking to sleep).

STEPS TO A GOOD NIGHT'S SLEEP

1. You should have appropriate expectations of your baby's sleep by now.
2. You are watching your baby's sensory world for over-stimulation, particularly before bedtime.
3. You have established a calming sleep zone.
4. You have addressed nutrition.
5. Your baby is healthy.
6. You have established a healthy day-sleep routine
7. You have set up healthy sleep associations.
8. You have dealt with separation issues.

CHAPTER 9

Sleep coaching

STEP 9: BREAK UNHEALTHY SLEEP HABITS BY TEACHING NEW SLEEP STRATEGIES AND CREATING BEDTIME BOUNDARIES

Johnny had started off as a good sleeper and his mom was sure she would not fall into the trap that other mothers did, of rocking their baby to sleep every night. So she would put Johnny down with his dummy and walk out the room. This had worked wonderfully for the first six months but now at seven months old, he was waking every 45 minutes to have his dummy popped back in. Julie was sure he wasn't hungry or thirsty and was following all the advice on bedtime routines and calming sleep space, but still Johnny woke up to 10 times a night. His mom had had enough and if this continued much longer, she was sure she would fall apart. She was ready to try anything.

If like Julie you have tried **everything**, you may feel ready to try **anything** to get a good night's sleep. At this point you may be inclined to let your baby cry it out if it means he will sleep through. On the other hand you may be holding on to the hope that you can change bad sleep habits without having to resort to that. The good news is that sleep coaching does not have to mean leaving your baby to cry for hours on end on his own.

By implementing healthy sleep habits **from the word go** by following the steps you have already learnt from the previous chapters in this book, you have already begun the process of sleep coaching without even realizing it. Be sure you have followed all the steps outlined in the first chapters of this book before you move on to the next step of sleep coaching. We are going to introduce you to two methods to coach your baby to modify his sleep – which is why we call this **sleep coaching**.

THINGS HAVE GONE WRONG

If you have accidentally fostered unhealthy sleep habits you are battling to resolve now, you are in good company. Falling into accidental parenting habits happens to many first time as well as experienced moms. At some point in the first year, most babies, even good sleepers go through periods of unsettledness at night. This may be due to illness, teething, hunger or a change of environment, such as a holiday. At these times, it may become necessary to assist your baby to fall asleep. The problem arises that when things return to normal and your baby's routine settles sufficient time may well have passed for bad habits to have developed.

As we learned in the chapter on sleep associations (Chapter 7), we all need a sensory cue to fall asleep, even as adults. If that cue is something your baby can use independently, such as sucking his thumb, he will be able to resettle himself at night. If, however, the sleep association is dependent on you, such as a feed, rocking or popping the dummy back in, your baby will continue to signal to you at night repeatedly to return and re-enact that sensory cue for him.

How frequently he needs assistance depends on how many times he is able to link sleep cycles and pass through the light sleep state back into a deep sleep state (see Chapter 1). If a small noise occurs when he is in the light sleep state, or if his nappy is cold as it would be in the early hours of the morning, he could well wake up. Some babies may stir every 45 minutes as they enter a light sleep state and parents may be woken repeatedly at these intervals throughout the night.

GETTING IT RIGHT

Because babies pass through light sleep states every 45 minutes at night (up to an hour in toddlers), it is possible for many babies to stir sufficiently to need assistance to resettle at night. You are not likely to prevent your baby stirring at night (due to sleep cycles) but you can and should teach your baby to go back to sleep without your assistance.

When should you consider sleep coaching?

The question is, at what age and under what circumstances is it reasonable to expect your baby to be able to resettle himself?

The skill of self-calming to put himself back to sleep is a developmental milestone that babies should achieve, in the same way as they reach the milestones of crawling or talking. This skill of self-calming is a vital one that you can reasonably expect of your baby from about four months of age. Bear in mind that between four and six months of age, some babies are still needing nutrition at night; therefore the basic need of hunger may cause a baby who settles himself well back to sleep most of the time, to wake (once a night) for nutrition.

Knowing that self-calming to sleep is a reasonable expectation, means that if all other reasons for night waking have been ruled out, it is quite reasonable to embark on a programme to teach your baby to sleep at night once he is **six months old**.

If your baby is younger than six months, refer to the sleep-coaching solutions in the troubleshooting chapter for your baby's age to set your baby up for good sleep habits.

SLEEP COACHING	**You can begin the process of sleep coaching if**

You can begin the process of sleep coaching if
- Your baby is healthy – illness or any other health issues have been ruled out by your health-care provider.
- Your baby is older than six months and his night waking is not due to hunger.

For your older baby the following principles form the basis of sleep modification, but each age group will present with different sleep challenges, so do refer to your baby's specific age chapter later on in the book.

The sense-able approach to sleep coaching

Remember how important it is for you to start early by implementing healthy sleep strategies from the word go. When sleep coaching is done correctly to meet your child's needs on all levels, especially his emotional needs, there should be no negative effects whatsoever. In fact, having a well-rested child with well-rested parents is an important part of creating a loving and secure home. Have the courage to be firm, without guilt or fear that your baby will resent or love you less. Remember that all possible causes for night waking need to be ruled out before you commence on this important journey.

THE THREE C'S OF SLEEP COACHING FOR PARENTS

Confidence

Research has shown that in the face of enormous trauma, such as an armed robbery or witnessing an attack by an animal, babies under three years of age only experience the event as traumatic and attach feelings of fear to similar circumstances if the mother communicates the emotion of fear during the event. If, while you are sleep coaching your baby, you stand over his cot with a look of fear in your eyes when he cries or with tears streaming down your face, he may experience the event as traumatic.

For this reason it is vital to communicate **confidence** and calm to your baby. When you start teaching him how to self-calm to sleep, he should see an emotion that makes him feel secure that you are comfortable with what you are doing. Inside you may be feeling very different and somewhat anxious as you begin, especially if you have tried other methods unsuccessfully. Remember, you are not going to leave your baby to cry uncontrollably on his own. You have ruled out any physical reasons for him not to sleep and have set the stage for healthy sleep. You are teaching your baby a new developmentally appropriate skill – that of going to sleep independently.

You will see from the steps below that there are two methods of doing this. Choose whichever you are confident doing. Both methods do work and have been tried and tested over many years of professional practice.

Consistency

Essential to teaching the new skill of self-soothing to sleep is consistency. It is no good to begin sleep coaching at bedtime only to relent later out of desperation and give your baby his 'crutch', for instance feeding him to sleep. The message that your baby receives in this case is that he must cry long and hard to have the old method reintroduced. The same applies to a toddler who may fall asleep in his mother's arms, but wake up in the night crying because he is no longer there, but is in his bed. Any inconsistencies will simply prolong the process of sleep coaching.

It is essential that you are consistent in your method of sleep coaching for **both** day and night sleeps, as well as when your baby wakes during the night. Do not embark on any form of sleep coaching/training until you feel you can follow through **consistently**. It will be confusing and unfair to your baby.

Collaboration

Collaboration literally means working together. Sleep coaching is an act of teamwork between you, your partner and your baby. It is absolutely essential that you **all** work together and do not undermine each other in the process. This is important especially because it has an impact on consistency: no matter which parent responds at night, you must both respond in the same way. It may be better for one parent do the sleep coaching to get 100% consistency. This is especially true if one parent is frequently away. But even if only one parent carries the load of actually doing the sleep coaching, both parents **must** buy in to the process. You will need your partner to be saying that you are doing the right thing and doing it well. In this way you feel supported and validated.

Ensure your partner reads this chapter and is fully behind you in this. If your partner is not supporting you and you do not have his **collaboration**, do not sleep train your baby yet. If a nanny or other caregiver is going to be involved with sleep coaching make sure she understands the process.

As you embark on the journey to modify your child's unhealthy sleep habits with confidence, consistency and collaboration you will find the pieces of this puzzle fall into place with greater ease than you expect. Keep reading!

SLEEP SECRET
The process of falling asleep unassisted is a skill that needs consolidation, so bear in mind that success comes only after a period of practice – don't give up!

BEFORE SLEEP COACHING – SET THE STAGE

- **Rule out** medical causes of night wakings with a visit to the doctor (Chapter 5).
- Establish a **day-sleep schedule**. Your baby's day sleep routine will be specific to your baby's age. Be sure to follow the Sleep Sense method to settle your baby to sleep (Chapter 6).
- Ensure your baby's **diet** is adequate for his age, with sufficient milk and age-appropriate solid food (Chapter 4).
- Your baby's **sleep zone** must support sleep and be a consistent and calming environment with white noise or lullabies (Chapter 3).
- Be sure to introduce a **sleep soother** that your baby can reach for to comfort himself (Chapter 7).

SLEEP COACHING PROCEDURE

Once you have checked all your baby's basic needs and have set the stage for sleep, you should be feeling confident enough to know that your baby **can** go to sleep on his own and stay asleep through the night.

After ruling out basic needs you are ready to embark on sleep coaching. When starting the programme follow the steps and advice strictly. Once you decide on a strategy, stick to it for at least one week before changing. Don't worry about being too rigid forever. As soon as your child's sleep improves you may become more flexible without confusing him!

Sensory input to assist sleep

In the late afternoon introduce some intense movement input. Spend 5 minutes with your baby rocking in a hammock, swinging on a swing or in your arms. Try to do this twice if your schedule allows. In this way you will provide 10 minutes of intense movement input.

If you have a busy toddler, encourage him to hang on the jungle gym and push and pull heavy objects. This sensory input is known as proprioception and is the reason we sleep so well after exercise.

Do not allow any television viewing after 4 pm as this has been found to disturb sleep.

Bedtime routine

Choose a bedtime that is reasonable for your baby's age. Any time between 6 pm and 7 pm is recommended until your child is about seven years old. Begin your bedtime routine one hour before your designated bedtime. This gives ample wind-down time in preparation for falling asleep.

- Begin the bedtime routine with a bath to which you may want to add some calming lavender or chamomile-scented bath products. Keep bath time quiet and calm with dimmed lights and few interactions. Toddlers, in particular, may find bath time very stimulating and splash and laugh in the bath. This is fine, as long as the environment and your voice remain quiet and calm. (For more specific toddler bedtime routines see the Chapter 15.)
- After his bath, wrap your child in a warm towel with a long deep hug, and move quietly with him into his sleep zone, which has been prepared for him.
- Give your baby a calming massage (good luck to you if you can achieve this with an active toddler – but try anyway!)
- Put a drop or two of **Rescue Remedy** (available from your pharmacy) onto your baby's wrist and temple pulse points, and gently rub it into the skin. **Rescue Remedy** is also most effective if dropped directly onto your baby's tongue. One drop per kilogram of body weight is a safe dosage to use. (You may need to mix it in a little bit of water to convince your toddler to take it!)
- Dress your child in warm, but comfortable nightclothes that are made of 100 % cotton.
- Stay in the sleep zone and encourage calming play such as paging through a

book or doing a puzzle. Keep stimulation to a minimum with absolutely no rough play or intense movement activities. Rather use deep pressure activities such as pushing or pulling heavy toys, massage and hugs.

LAST FEED AND GOOD NIGHT
- After a short period of quiet time, give him his last feed – breast or bottle – in your arms, until he is drowsy.
- If you have to stand up and rock him until he is drowsy, that is fine. This may take some time, so don't stress; enjoy this special time with your baby.
- Make shushing sounds or sing a calming lullaby until he is calm and relaxed.
- Put him into his bed gently (remember, not head first), encourage the use of his sleep soother or blanky, and quietly and confidently walk out of his sleep zone.

Sleep coaching: six months and older still in a cot
In all likelihood if your baby or toddler has developed a habit whereby he is dependent on you to fall sleep, he will protest within minutes (probably even seconds!) of you leaving the room. This is where the hard bit comes in. Accept that your baby is going to cry, but you are going to control how long he will cry for and will be there for him every step of the way. There are two methods of handling this: neither one is better than the other – do what feels right for you at the time. You know your baby intimately, don't worry about making the wrong decision, you will know when the time comes which method to use. One thing though, remember to be consistent and stick to one method for at least a week. Try not to give your child any mixed messages, otherwise no sleep modification programme will work.

METHOD ONE: STAYING WITH YOUR BABY
This sensible method works well if you feel confident to stay with your baby while he is learning to put himself to sleep. Since you are not leaving your baby and are conveying a message of consistency and confidence your baby will feel secure, not abandoned so there is less risk of him crying hysterically or vomiting which is frequently encountered with the controlled crying methods of sleep training.

The first night
- Once you leave the room, first listen to your baby's cry. If he is moaning or chatting, do not respond – give him the opportunity to self-soothe to sleep. This goes for the middle of the night too – don't respond unless he really cries.
- If he is really crying, go back into his sleep zone, and sit in a chair next to him. Put your hand gently, but firmly on him (anywhere on his body will do). Don't move your hand and don't talk, except to say 'shshsh'. You are using three sensory inputs to support your baby: he can **see** you, he can **feel** you and he can **hear** you. Sit with him until he goes to sleep. Do not look worried or concerned, rather just close your eyes and continue to say 'shshssh'. Encourage

the use of his *sleep soother* and help him to lie back down if he wants to stand up. Continue to sit next to him with your hand on his body. If he is expecting to be fed or rocked to sleep he will most definitely cry. Don't be swayed by this, it is going to be hard, but keep calm and persevere. Your baby may cry for a long time – up to an hour (or even longer). You should simply sit quietly with him and appear calm and confident. This may be easier to do if you don't make eye contact. He will eventually fall asleep.

- Repeat this procedure each time he wakes during the first night, always offering his sleep soother to him first.

The second night

The **next night** start the routine in the same way. When you put your baby into his bed and he begins to cry, respond to him immediately (unless it is a moan or a whimper), but this time, do not touch him. Sit next to his bed and just say "shshsh" repeatedly. He experiences two sensory inputs: **seeing** you and **hearing** you. Do this every time he wakes the second night, no matter how long it takes. The second night is difficult for you as you will be feeling very tired and fragile as a result of the night before, but the upside is that your baby will be getting the idea of putting himself to sleep without much assistance. The trick is to be consistent. Repeat the same procedure (no touch, but reassuring words) at every waking throughout the night.

The third night

On the **third night** start the bedtime routine in exactly the same way, offering him his sleep soother and walking out of the room calmly and confidently. When he cries, respond, but this time simply sit quietly next to his bed (no touch, and no sound) until he falls asleep. This time you have removed the tactile and auditory crutches you were giving your baby. Repeat this at every waking throughout the night.

The final phase

- On the **fourth night**, if he cries, return to his sleep zone, offer him his sleep soother, then stand near the door until he falls asleep. Repeat this procedure each time he wakes throughout the night.
- Finally on the **fifth night**, listen to see if he can put himself to sleep independently. If not, respond to his cries, offer him his sleep soother and then stand just outside his sleep zone, occasionally saying "shshsh" while he cries. Repeat this at every waking throughout the night.
- By this stage, your baby has learnt how to fall asleep independently both at bedtime, and during the night when he wakes
- One week down the line, just when you think you've got it right, he may have a 'protest night' where he will be very unsettled. Don't worry, if you expect it, you can handle it – simply go back to the beginning and start again! This time he should settle for good.

METHOD TWO: LEAVING YOUR BABY FOR SHORT PERIODS OF TIME

This method of sleep coaching allows you to pick up your baby when he is crying and comfort him until he is calm, but it differs from the first method in that you actually leave the room for short periods of time from the outset. Some parents may feel uncomfortable with separating from their babies, so method one is preferable for them. But for other parents, short periods of separation from their babies while sleep coaching work better for them as they cannot bear the thought of sitting alongside their crying baby. If you feel that you could possibly harm your baby physically (out of sheer exhaustion and frustration) this is the method of choice for you as you are able to step away from the situation for very short periods of time in order to catch your breath and re-focus on the goal in sight.

Follow the same bedtime routine and put your baby to bed when he is calm and relaxed. Make sure he has his sleep soother and quietly leave the room. If he cries, proceed as follows:

- First listen to his cry. If he is moaning or chatting, do not respond – give him the opportunity to self-soothe to sleep. This goes for the middle of the night too – don't respond unless he really cries. If so, return to his sleep zone, offer him his sleep soother and put your hand firmly onto his body, saying "shshsh" for a minute or two. Avoid eye contact and keep things quiet and calm.

- If he stops crying, continue with this input for another minute or two, then leave the room. If he continues to cry, pick him up and comfort him. Do this in a calm and quiet manner, simply saying "shshsh". Stay with him until he has stopped crying, and has become drowsy. This may take a while, so be patient. You may need to help him to get drowsy again by rocking and holding him close to you. As soon as he has stopped crying, and is calm and drowsy, place him back in his bed (remember, not head first). Encourage the use of his sleep soother, place your hand firmly onto his body, saying "shshsh", for another few seconds, then leave the room.

- If he is simply moaning and thrashing about in his bed after this, leave him be, but if he is begins to cry, wait for **one** minute before you respond to him. Return to the sleep zone, and try settling him by placing your hand somewhere on his body and saying "shshsh". Encourage the use of his sleep soother. Avoid eye contact and keep things calm. If he stops crying, continue with this input for another minute or two, then leave the room. If he continues to cry, pick him up and comfort him. Encourage the use of his sleep soother. Do this in a calm and quiet manner, simply saying "shshsh". Stay with him until he has stopped crying, and has become drowsy. You may need to help him to get drowsy again by rocking and holding him close to you. As soon as he has stopped crying, and is calm and drowsy, place him back in his bed. Place your hand firmly onto his body saying "shshsh" for another few seconds, encourage the use of his sleep soother, then leave the room.

SLEEP SECRET
All methods of sleep training entail some fussing and crying. You are teaching your baby a new skill and breaking old expectations. While some crying is unavoidable the 'Crying it out' method is not advisable, as it can make your baby feel abandoned and emotionally insecure.

- If he is moaning, leave him be, but if he begins to cry, wait for **two** minutes before you respond to him by returning to the sleep zone and repeating the calming process once more.
- Continue in this manner, increasing the period of time you spend away from the sleep zone by **one** minute each time up to six minutes or until he eventually falls asleep, whichever comes first.
- Keep the maximum time spent away from the sleep zone to six minutes. This process may need to be repeated so do stay calm and focused.
- When your baby wakes during the night, respond to his cries, comfort him until he is calm, then repeat the procedure, starting with one minute of separation with the first waking, and increasing the period of separation by one minute with each subsequent waking (up to six minutes)

Some babies gag and may even vomit whilst they are crying. So do not be alarmed if this happens. You **know** your baby is not sick (you would not be doing sleep coaching if this was the case), so if it is not your time to go back to the sleep zone, do not respond. When you do return to the sleep zone, don't make a big issue of cleaning up, simply place a clean towel under your baby.

As you can imagine, there will be much toing and froing in and out of the sleep zone for the first night at least. But give it some time (usually a night or two), and you will see that your baby will soon learn to *put himself to* sleep and go *back to sleep* independently.

Do expect a protest night about a week down the line. Stay calm and focused, stick to the plan, and he will soon re-settle.

If things don't quite go according to plan

If you have successfully coached your baby to put himself to sleep on his own at bedtime, chances are that he *will* be able to self-calm and go back to sleep independently during the course of the night. Occasionally, however, this is not the case, and you may find that even though your *bedtime blues* are over, your baby continues to wake repeatedly throughout the night. All he needs to re-settle is your presence in the sleep zone, and perhaps a quick touch onto his body. All very well, it's a very quick wake, and seconds later you are back in bed asleep. But the fact of the matter is that you are having a very *broken* night's sleep. Keep going like this for weeks or even months, and it won't be long before you begin to fall to pieces from exhaustion.

Since your baby is well, not hungry or cold and has successfully learnt to **put himself to sleep at bedtime** through a process of sleep modification, all he may need is an opportunity to self-soothe during the night. This method involves four steps:

- When he cries, do not respond immediately; rather *give him a chance* to see if he can settle himself. If he is simply moaning or talking, leave him be.
- If he is crying, wait for **one minute** before you respond to him by returning to his sleep zone and encouraging his sleep soother.

- With each waking increase the **listening time** by one minute, giving him good opportunity to use his newly learnt skill of self-soothing.
- Take note of the time you waited before responding at the **last** waking of the night. This is the time you are going to wait before responding at the first waking the **following** night.

Remember, when you go to your baby, always encourage the use of his sleep soother Keep going – you will be amazed how quickly your baby will learn to self-calm in the middle of the night.

Sleep coaching: Toddler to preschooler

As soon as your toddler outgrows his cot and makes the transition into a 'big bed', there may be some high jinks at bedtime. Some children simply find that this newfound freedom is a wonderful excuse for prolonged bedtimes, plus frequent visits to mom and dad's bedroom throughout the night! If your toddler begins to negotiate or protest or jumps out of bed within minutes of you leaving the room asking for a snack or water or that you lie with him, adopt these simple sleep strategies to teach him how to put himself to sleep.

Back to bed

Walk your toddler back to back to bed, without admonishing him or raising your voice. Stay calm, confident and focused. Encourage the use of his familiar sleep soother (blanky, teddy, thumb or put his dummy in his hand) and follow these steps:

- Respond by **acknowledging** his request: Say to him: 'I know you want … (me to lie with you/a snack).'
- **Empathise** so he feels understood by mirroring his request: Say to him: 'I would love to … (lie down with you/get you a snack).'
- Give a **reason**: Say to him: 'But I/you can't … (lie with you because I have my own bed/have a snack in your bed because you will choke).'
- Offer an **alternative** solution. Say to him: 'Rather lie here with your special teddy, and I'll sit on the bed next to you.'
- Set a **boundary**: Say to him 'If you lie down and go to sleep, I will sit with you until you fall asleep.'
- Give a **consequence.** Say to him: 'If you get up again, I will have to leave.'

Follow through

For as long as your toddler stays in bed and makes an effort to be quiet and go to sleep, sit with him until he falls asleep (no matter how long it takes, so be prepared for this). You must stick to your end of the deal if he sticks to his.

If he breaks his end of the deal, by getting up, jumping on the bed, asking for juice or whatever his tactic is, you must remind him about the deal you made and offer him a chance to try again. If he resists, get up, leave the room and close the door so that he can't follow. It is important that he remains in his room so if he is able to open the door himself install a latch. Don't worry about leaving him behind a closed door. You are simply making sure that his room is containing him much the same as he was contained in his cot before. This is why it is important to have a night-light on and to make his room a safe environment for him. From outside the room, tell him you will return when he gets back into bed.

Go back in

As soon as you see or hear him get onto his bed, OR after **one** minute of crying (whatever happens first), go back into his room quietly and calmly. Resist the temptation to raise your voice. If he is crying, calm him down with a hug, encourage the use of his sleep soother, wait until he has stopped crying, then re-negotiate with him. (Remember to acknowledge and empathise with his request, then give him a reason, a boundary and a consequence).

Follow through, then go back in

Leave the room if he does not comply with the boundary you have offered him (which is to stay with him until he falls asleep provided he lies in his bed). Close the door. Return to him immediately if he does get back into bed, and praise him for listening to you. Reward him by staying with him until he falls asleep.

If he cries and bangs on the door, wait for **two** minutes before you return to re-negotiate with him. Remember to stay calm and focused, never raise your voice and offer him lots of calming stimuli such as a hug and his sleep soother each time. He needs to be calm again before you can re-negotiate with him. Be prepared for this to take some time.

Keep going

Keep going in this manner – return to him as soon as he is back in bed, OR if he will not stay in his bed and bangs on the door, **increase** the period of time before you respond to him by one minute each time until he eventually falls asleep.

Repeat the procedure each time he wakes during the first night. If he complies with your boundary (by staying in his bed) always reward him by staying with him as you have promised (no matter how tedious you may find this in the middle of the night) until he falls asleep. If he will not comply (by jumping out of bed and running away), leave the room, close the door and leave him for **one** minute until you return quietly and calmly to re-negotiate! If you do have to leave the room, **increase** the period of time by one minute each time, until he eventually falls asleep. Remember you need to create a **firm consistent boundary** for a child of this age.

The next step

By the second or third night, your toddler has probably realized that if he does as you ask him (which is to stop the high jinks at sleep time), you *will* sit with him on the bed until he goes to sleep at bedtime, and if he wakes during the night.

When this is consistently happening, it is time to move to the next step. Be patient, it may take time to get to this step.

Begin bedtime in exactly the same way, and if he comes out of his room, tell him (by acknowledging, empathising and reasoning, with a boundary and a consequence) that you will no longer be sitting on the bed with him, but will rather be sitting in a chair alongside the bed. As before, complete your negotiation with him. If he complies with your boundary (which is to stay in his bed and go to sleep) you will stay in his room with him, but you will be in the chair. If he does not comply with your boundary, then follow the same procedure as before by going out of the room and closing the door. Continue with the programme as you did before, until he falls asleep.

When he is happy to stay in his bed and go to sleep as long as you are sitting in the chair (at bedtime and when he wakes in the night), move to the next step. Bear in mind it may take you a few nights to achieve this – be patient, loving and consistent.

Move further away

Move the chair away from his bed to another part of the room as close to the door as possible. Repeat the sleep coaching steps as above until he is happy to go to sleep in his bed with you sitting in the sleep zone apart from him.

The next step is to move the chair out of the room. At bedtime, simply 'linger' in the room, maybe even stepping into the bathroom for a second or two (always reassure him that you will be back) before returning to 'linger' once more. Repeat the sleep modification steps as above until he is happy to go to sleep in his bed as long as you are 'lingering' around.

Leaving the room

The final step (this step may have taken you as little as a few days to reach, or it may be a week down the line by now) is to tell him you need to leave the room for a minute to perform a task. Reassure him that when you are finished your task you promise to return. Do as you have promised and return. Don't forget to praise him each time you return if he has stayed in his bed. Keep popping in and out, but gradually increase the amount of time you spend out of his room. Repeat the sleep modification steps as above until he is happy to fall asleep in his bed as long as you continue to pop in and out.

After a few nights of this you will return after your first absence to find him asleep. At last! Your toddler has learnt the new technique of falling asleep independently.

Caring for yourself during sleep coaching

Sleep coaching is exhausting and the key to its success is to focus on the goal at the end of it all. Accept that you will be tired and frustrated at times, but try not to get bogged down in the immediate drama of the moment, and rather look at your long-term goal. Try these simple strategies:

> SLEEP SECRET
> Like babies, once toddlers are sleep trained, they frequently have a protest night a week down the line. Expect it and handle it in the same way as when you were coaching him.

- Decide on an appropriate time to commence sleep modification – not when you are caught up in work deadlines, or your caregiver is on leave. Allow for time beforehand to set the stage for sleep before rushing into sleep coaching.
- If possible, arrange for a day's leave on either end of your weekend to allow consistent time for sleep coaching to work. A lot of the 'hard work' will be over by the time you have to function normally at work again.
- Try to sleep once a day while your baby sleeps, preferably at a time between 12 noon and 3 pm, when your natural circadian rhythms will allow you to have the most rested period of sleep. It is essential that you are rested for the night ahead. If you are not prepared, you will be more likely to give up or be inconsistent out of sheer exhaustion.
- If possible, take shifts with your partner to allow you to have some undisturbed sleep somewhere along the line to recharge!
- If you have other children or demands, try to elicit help and support from family or an au pair for the first few days of sleep modification, so that you can focus exclusively on the sleep coaching. Reassure your other children that you will make it up to them later – don't forget to do this!
- Earmark a reward for yourself and the caregivers involved in the sleep coaching programme at the end of it all – a massage, or a special dinner, or the purchase of a coveted item.

Sleep zone

As far as possible try to **never leave the sleep zone with your baby** at night. You will teach your baby that this is where he sleeps when it is bedtime, and it is dark. If you are sleep coaching your baby during the day, it is fine to leave the sleep zone if you have been unsuccessful after an hour has passed. Take him somewhere pleasurable, such as into the garden (keep it quiet and calm), then return to the sleep zone to try again about half an hour later. As you know, instituting a day-sleep routine is part of sleep coaching, but don't stress unduly if the day routine is a bit higgledy-piggledy until everything falls into place. This may take a few days to get right.

Picking up your baby

While sleep coaching your baby there may be times when he needs a cuddle or to be comforted in your arms. This is appropriate and meets not only your baby's emotional needs but yours too. At times it may make the crying worse. For instance, picking your baby up but not feeding him (if you are trying to break a night feeding habit), may enrage him so much (because he is expecting to be fed), that it might make him cry even harder! He may also become more upset if he is already overtired and over stimulated. Picking him up may also give him mixed messages in terms of boundaries and consequences and thereby make the process of sleep coaching harder in the long run. You will soon be able to tell if picking up your baby makes him feel better or worse.

SLEEP SECRET
If you are sleep coaching your baby during the day and an hour has passed without success, leave the sleep zone; spend some happy time together.

What about medication to solve sleep problems?

There are drugs available that induce sleep in babies. They should never be given unless prescribed by your paediatrician, as they can be dangerous owing to their sedative effects. The advantage of these drugs is that in appropriate doses they will most likely result in sleep and will give you a much-needed night of respite. In certain cases, especially if you are suffering from postnatal depression, or if your fatigue is becoming dangerous for your health, a doctor may decide that the positive effect of a night's sleep for the you far outweighs any negative effect on your baby that may be associated with sleep medication. Nevertheless, there are three reasons why you should approach medicating sleep problems with caution:

- Do not be mislead into thinking that medication will solve your baby's sleep problem. Most babies start to wake again when the dose of medication is reduced or stopped. Your baby has not learnt a new skill of self-soothing and the old reasons for unhealthy sleep habits still exist.
- Sleep medications, particularly in high doses, may result in a 'hang over' the next morning. Your baby may be drowsy and somewhat irritable during the day leading to feeding and behavioural problems.
- Some babies respond unpredictably to medication. They become more awake and may become agitated and irritable. If this happens you will have a tough night ahead of you.

SUMMARY OF SLEEP COACHING

The **goal** of sleep coaching is to teach your baby to fall asleep independently. To achieve this, you must be confident, consistent and have the collaboration of your partner. The **process** of sleep coaching involves

- Equipping your baby with a healthy, independent sleep association
- Following a strict bedtime routine
- Following a sleep programme of choice, and sticking to it.
- A time period of one to five nights and may be followed by a protest night one week down the line.

STEPS TO A GOOD NIGHT'S SLEEP

1. You have appropriate expectation of your baby's sleep.
2. You observe your baby's sensory world for over-stimulation.
3. You have established a calming sleep zone.
4. You have ensured your baby's nutrition is adequate for sleep.
5. Your are sure that your baby is healthy.
6. You have established a healthy day-sleep routine.
7. You have taught your baby healthy sleep associations.
8. You have dealt with separation issues.
9. You have now helped your baby establish healthy sleep habits.

Sleep diary after Sleep sense

Having completed the **Sleep sense 9 steps**, we suggest you take the time to record your baby's sleep patterns for at least two consecutive nights. Compare your record with the Sleep diary before **Sleep sense** to track your progress and see just how far you have come on the journey to a good night's sleep. Well done!

Week date: _____   **Baby's age:** _____

1. Where do you prepare your baby for sleep? In his sleep zone, the car or anywhere in the house? _____

2. Note relevant points about the sleep zone: lighting, cot, bedding etc. _____

Awake: Leave all blocks when your baby is awake blank; this will highlight how much time your baby spends awake between sleeps during the day.

Trying to settle or fighting sleep: Put a diagonal line through all blocks when you are trying to get your baby to sleep. In the space below these blocks record what interventions you are implementing to calm your baby or get him to sleep.

Asleep: Shade all blocks when your baby is asleep. Under each shaded block you can record where and how your baby sleeps, for example very restless, dead still, noisy etc.

DAY	6	7	8	9	10	11	12	1 pm	2	3	4	5	6	7	8	9	10	11	12	1 am	2	3	4	5
1																								
2																								
3																								
4																								
5																								
6																								

Quick relief for tired parents

Quick relief for tired parents – newborns

In the first few weeks of your baby's life you will experience a roller coaster of feelings. At times you are so elated and delighted by your precious bundle that you can hardly stop yourself from simply gazing in awe at your baby and drinking in that newborn smell. At other times, you may feel quite anxious and overwhelmed. If you are recovering from a traumatic birth or a caesarean section, you may even feel 'spaced out' and groggy from the effect of medication you are taking for pain. Of course, feeling totally out of your depth with elevated anxiety levels are also very much a reality in the early days. For most new parents, the shocking realization of how little sleep you are actually getting will dawn within the first two weeks after birth and tears of exhaustion will override or amplify any joy, pain or anxiety you may be feeling.

WHAT TO EXPECT IN TERMS OF SLEEP AT THIS STAGE

- In the early days your newborn may have his day and night muddled up, feeding more frequently at night and sleeping all day.
- At this very young age, expect your newborn to spend little time awake unless it is for a feed. Do not worry about stimulation or play time when he is awake, rather let him eat, clear his digestive system with a wind and a bowel motion (not always), have a cuddle and return to sleep.
- Your newborn cannot be expected to sleep through the night and will wake frequently to feed.
- Try to sleep during the day when your baby sleeps so you do not become too exhausted.
- By six weeks old, your baby's feeding routine should be settling down, and he should be sleeping for at least one longer stretch at night and waking to feed at least 4-hourly for all his other feeds.

GETTING IT RIGHT: THE BASICS

Since disturbed sleep owing to frequent night feeds are part of this early stage of development; there is not much you can do about lack of sleep at this point. However, if your baby is unusually unsettled and rarely sleeps for longer than 15 minutes at a time during the day or night, or both, you must address the following issues, and get some strategies into place right away. These strategies will help you deal with the problem at hand, as well as help you to foster long-lasting healthy sleep habits.

Rule out illness

If your baby is unusually irritable and not feeding well, read Chapter 5 carefully and visit your doctor to be sure that your baby is not ill

Rule out other health issues

Your baby may be unsettled and be labelled 'colicy'. **Colic** is a term that is bandied about and used as a broad umbrella term for **all** kinds of distressed behaviour in the early days. Read Chapter 5 carefully to exclude issues such as Gastro-oesophageal reflux, which may be causing your baby to be very restless.

Consider your baby's nutritional needs

If your baby is waking very frequently at night at this stage, consider the following:
- Babies do need to feed almost as frequently at night as during the day in the early days. Feed him when he is hungry.
- If you are breast feeding, remember that your milk supply takes at least six weeks to fully establish itself. It is important that you look after yourself properly at this stage and breast feed on demand to ensure an adequate milk supply.
- If you are bottle feeding and your baby wakes more frequently than four hourly at night, consider changing his formula to a more filling one – check with your clinic sister or paediatrician before you do this.
- Your baby may demand one or two cluster feeds which are feeds close together in the early part of the evening – encourage this if it is helping him to sleep for a slightly longer stretch later.

IMPORTANT NOTE

Try to avoid supplementary or complementary feeding at this age, but if your baby is not thriving, discuss this issue with your clinic sister or paediatrician, and follow the guidelines as laid out in Chapter 4, page 43.

BOOSTING BREAST MILK SUPPLY

As you muddle along during these early weeks, adjusting to parenthood, you may not be eating a balanced diet. Snatched meals of convenience food or take-outs do not provide the essential nutrients your body needs for the effort of producing milk. Consider taking supplements high in lucerne and alfalfa protein, with the right amount of vitamin B. These are available in tablet form, or as a tea. A tonic made from blackthorn berries is a refreshing and energizing drink when mixed with a little water or as an ingredient of 'Jungle Juice' (see recipe on the next page). You can drink two litres a day to enhance milk production.

GETTING IT RIGHT: SETTING THE STAGE

Your baby's sensory world has a huge effect on his mood and sleep. Remember that your new baby has a very limited threshold for stimulation.

The sleep zone

At this young age, let your baby sleep wherever it suits you most: in his room in a crib, in your room in a crib or in a co-sleeper nest in your bed. Provided you keep the sleep zone quiet and calm (see Chapter 3), don't worry about creating bad sleeping habits at this stage.

Help your baby to sleep during the day

The busy world around your baby can overwhelm him very easily, particularly if he is tired. This will make him grumpy and irritable and he will be more likely to resist sleep when he is in this state.

SLEEP SECRET
To ensure that your baby is getting enough to eat, weigh him regularly, and check that he has six to seven wet nappies in a 24-hour period.

- Prevent over-tiredness by limiting his awake time between sleeps to 45-60 minutes (see page 61).
- Do not stress about enforcing day routines at this young age. Rather watch how long he has been awake and learn to recognize his signals indicating tiredness (see page 25) to guide him into a day-sleep pattern.
- **Use sense-able sensory steps to help him:** Mimic the calming world of the womb in your newborn's environment to prevent over-stimulation. Try these sensory steps:
  - *Touch* Keep him swaddled in a stretchy 100 % cotton blanket all the time except during nappy changes.
  - *Visual* Dim his room and cover the front of the pram to block out bright light at sleep times.
  - *Sound* Use white noise at sleep time to help him settle and sleep deeper and longer.
  - *Movement* Rock your baby or push him in a pram to settle him if he is fractious and is fighting sleep. Use a sling to keep your baby close to you. A baby hammock is nice to get a fractious baby to sleep.
  - *Smells and taste* Your breast milk and mummy smells are calming and help to induce sleep.

GETTING IT RIGHT AT BEDTIME

Your baby will not be in a routine and will be sleeping a lot but if he gets over-tired he will fight sleep and become 'colicky'. If your baby is fractious and won't settle to sleep, try these ideas:

• Help him to sleep regularly during the day by avoiding sensory overload.

• If your baby is unsettled at sleep-time keep him swaddled, and hold him against you until he is asleep and settled. Place him into his bed gently (not head first). Do not be concerned about 'spoiling' your baby at this stage.

• If he wakes within 15 minutes of going to sleep, re-swaddle him, encourage him to suck on his or your finger or a dummy, and gently pat him. You may want to try offering him a quick 'top up' feed at this point to see if that will help settle him. If this feed makes him worse, you have most likely over-fed him and caused him to become uncomfortable, so don't be tempted to try it again.

• If he remains unsettled, pick him up gently and rock and hold him close to you until he falls asleep.

GETTING IT RIGHT AT NIGHT

If your baby continually wakes at night and he is not hungry or ill follow these age appropriate guidelines:

• Feed him when he wakes at night if more than 2 hours have passed since the last feed.

• Your baby may wake as often as three-hourly at night for a feed in the early days.

• If he wakes after an hour or so (when he doesn't need a feed), re-swaddle him, pat him gently but firmly, and let him suck on your finger or a dummy to get him back to sleep. Try not to pick him up if he is just niggling, as this may wake him up fully and he may expect a feed (even if he doesn't need it). Obviously, if he is crying, pick him up gently and comfort him. Rock him and hold him until he goes back to sleep.

• Don't wake your baby to feed him at night unless you have been instructed to by your health-care worker, for example if he was premature, or is not gaining weight.

• Keep night feeds, between 6 pm and 6 am, very quiet and calm by remaining in the sleep zone, keeping the light dimmed, and limiting interaction.

• If your baby is sleeping exceptionally well at night, or is only waking once at this age – count your blessings! Provided he is healthy and is gaining weight, you do not need to be concerned.

COMMON SLEEP ISSUES FROM BIRTH TO SIX WEEKS
Difficulty settling when put down to sleep

My son is now 2 weeks old. Everything seemed to be going fine until a couple of days ago when he seemed to develop real 'separation anxiety'. He is a contented baby as long as he is being held. We have tried putting him down drowsy – but he wakes up and starts fussing. He falls asleep quite happily provided he is being cuddled – or lying on top of us. If we then transfer him into his cot he wakes up – no matter how deep the sleep seems before we move him. He resists swaddling, and kicks his blankets off and then fusses until someone picks him up again. This happens during the day and night. In desperation I have ended up letting him sleep next to me – so that both of us can at least get some rest, but I am worried that this will create a lasting habit we won't be able to break.

Sleep solution: Your baby is still so tiny; don't worry about starting any bad habits when he is so young. At this stage, he needs his sleep more than he needs to learn how to put himself to sleep unassisted, so do what it takes to get him to fall asleep. Ensure that he is not over-stimulated at all, and watch that his awake time is no longer than 60 minutes (including feeding time). If he is fussing when you put him down, keep your hand on him for deep pressure to help him feel contained. Keep him swaddled for all sleeps. Persevere with this, even if he appears to resist swaddling – he will learn to like it. Make sure that his hands are close to his face so that he can suck on them if needs be. Check with your paediatrician to exclude any health issues such as reflux, which can cause babies to be unsettled when they lie down.

> **SLEEP SECRET**
> Your young baby does not necessarily need to always feed before he sleeps. Bear in mind that some sleeps might happen before a feed is due. If this is the case, let him sleep and feed him when he wakes up.

Resisting day sleeps

For the last two days, my five-week-old will only sleep for half an hour twice during the day, and resists all other sleeps despite being tired and niggley most of the time. She is a colicky baby and will only fall asleep in my arms and even then it is not for long. When we have days like this, we don't sleep well at night either. I tried getting her drowsy and putting her down but she starts screaming. Please help as I don't want to land up in a situation where I have to rock her to sleep until she is two years old. Is she too young to sleep train?

Sleep solution: It is always a good idea to take your baby to the paediatrician to be sure that you are not missing a health issue. If she has a clean bill of health, you can begin to modify her sleeping patterns. You must regulate how long she is awake between sleeps. If she is awake for long she will become over-stimulated and will struggle to fall asleep without a lot of help such as rocking or feeding. This may be why she appears to be colicky, as sensory overload or over-stimulation mimics the signs of colic.

She will be able to manage with at most an hour (60 minutes) of awake time at this age. Take note of the time she wakes and fit in her feed, nappy change and a tiny bit of interaction during that hour. You will see that she will start to give you signals that she is tired such as looking away from you or fidgeting and hiccupping (don't mistake these for signs of colic). At this point, wrap her up in a stretchy 100 % cotton swaddle blanket, sit quietly with her in her quiet and darkened sleep zone. Hold her close, gently rock her and make no eye contact until she is drowsy then put her into her crib.

Put on a CD of white noise or lulling music to drown out background noise that might be troubling her and let her go to sleep. If she fusses, place your hand on her body (avoid tickling her) or let her suck on your finger or a dummy. If she has not settled within a few minutes, and begins to cry, pick her up gently and rock her (a sling is most useful in this instance) until she is drowsy, then try again to put her into her bed. If she continues to cry and is not asleep within 15 minutes, then hold her and rock her until she is asleep. Once she is fast asleep, place her gently (not head first) into her bed.

Although you don't want to develop habits for falling asleep, it is more important at this stage for her to sleep than to worry about how it happens. Little babies need to be held a lot at this stage, so don't worry about bad habits just yet. If you think about it, you are already sleep coaching her by modifying how you put her to bed! It is not advisable to leave her to cry at this stage.

COLIC

It is helpful to understand 'colic' in the context of over stimulation. This will help you watch your baby's sensory load to avert this restlessness.

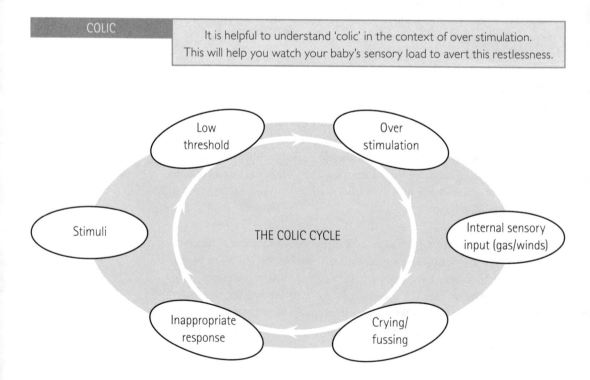

Sleepy baby

My newborn baby seems to sleep so much. I have never really heard her cry, she only stirs and whimpers when she is hungry, or has a dirty nappy, and settles straight back to sleep as soon as I have fed her, which is about every three hours. Is there something wrong with her?

Sleep solution: Most newborns are very sleepy and will only wake if there is something troubling them such as hunger or a wet nappy. She is obviously very content for now, so enjoy this quiet time with her – she will be sure to 'wake up' by the time she is 6 weeks old! Make sure she is not ill (see Chapter 5, page 51) and weigh her every week to ensure she is growing. If she is showing no signs of becoming more alert by the time she is four to six weeks of age, it is advisable to take her to a paediatrician for a full check-up.

Sleep deprivation contributes to postnatal depression

There is overwhelming evidence that in a sleep deprived state mothers are more susceptible to post-natal depression. If your baby is not sleeping well and you suffer from any of the symptoms below, seek help. The Postnatal Depression Support Association of South Africa (PNDSA) provides education and information to health professionals and care providers and to the public. You will find support and appropriate referrals by contacting PNDSA or speaking to your doctor.

If you feel:
- Out of control, frustrated and very irritable
- That you are not the kind of mother that you want to be
- Anxious and worried most of the time
- Scared or panicky
- Sad or miserable
- Unable to laugh or to feel joy
- Unable to cope
- Afraid to be alone
- Unusually tearful
- As though you are going crazy an/or

If you have:
- Difficulty sleeping
- No sex drive
- Thoughts about harming yourself or your baby

You may be suffering from postnatal depression.
Please seek help.
Tel: PNDSA
Help lines: 082 882 0072 or 083 309 3960 or Tel/Fax: (021) 797 4498
e-mail: liz@pndsa.co.za

Quick relief for tired parents – six weeks to four months

This is often the hardest time for you. You have been sleep-deprived for six weeks, and the novelty of night feeds may be somewhat jaded by now! It is unlikely that your baby is sleeping for very long periods of time at night, and the effects of long-term broken sleep begin to take their toll on your mood and your coping strategies. If your baby is fussy during the day as well, you will be struggling.

WHAT TO EXPECT IN TERMS OF SLEEP AT THIS STAGE

- It may seem to you that many babies are sleeping through at this stage, but that is not always the case. Most babies are still waking for at least one feed during the night.
- Between six weeks and four months of age, your baby should start to have one long stretch at night of six to eight hours without a feed. She is unlikely to be able to stretch longer than three to four hourly between feeds thereafter.
- If you are helping your baby to find self-calming strategies (see Chapter 7), such as sucking on her hands or holding her hands together, she may well start to self-sooth back to sleep when she stirs at night, provided she is not hungry.
- By ten weeks of age, your baby's day routine should be settling down, but she will still only manage to handle small amounts of stimulation and awake time.
- You should aim for a bedtime of between 6 and 7 pm. You can expect your baby to wake once between midnight and 5 am and then again in the morning between 5 and 7 am (depending on what time she fed in the night).

GETTING IT RIGHT: THE BASICS

If your baby is generally unsettled and never sleeps for long periods of time during the day or night, and is still waking frequently to feed at night, you need to address the following issues and get some sleep strategies into place right away. These strategies will help you deal with the problem at hand, as well as assist you to foster long-lasting healthy sleep habits:

RULE OUT ILLNESS
If your baby is unusually irritable and not feeding, read Chapter 5 carefully or visit your doctor to be sure that she is not ill.

Rule out other health issues

If your baby is very restless, especially at night read Chapter 5, page 52 carefully to exclude issues such as gastro-oesophageal reflux. It is unlikely that your baby is teething at this young age, so don't blame restless nights on teeth. She will 'find' her hands at around ten weeks of age, and will love to suck on them to effectively self-calm, so don't confuse this sign with teething.

Your baby's nutritional needs

If your baby is still feeding frequently during the night or is not able to last for one stretch of at least five to six hours without needing a feed, hunger may well be contributing to her lack of sleep. It is important that you read Chapter 4, page 41. In the meanwhile, follow these simple guidelines:

- If you are bottle feeding, know what she weighs to ensure she is drinking sufficient volume of milk.
- Check that she is having six to seven wet nappies during a 24 hour period, especially if you are breastfeeding.
- Don't be tempted to let her sleep for long periods of time (more than four hours) during the day without a feed.
- If you are breastfeeding, ensure that you look after yourself by having enough rest and by eating properly. Make up some 'jungle juice' (see recipe, page 105.) and drink it throughout the day, or ask your pharmacist or clinic nurse to recommend appropriate vitamin supplements to boost your milk supply.
- Consider supplementary or complementary feeding if your baby is still unsettled (see page 43).
- Expect a growth spurt at around six to eight weeks of age, and again at around three months of age when you might have to feed more frequently for about 24-48 hours.
- If your baby seems unsettled in the early evening and wakes frequently before midnight, you could try cluster feeding (feed frequently in the period of time between bath time and bedtime) or offer her a top-up bottle of expressed breast milk or formula when you put her down in the evening.
- If she wakes within an hour of going to sleep at night, offer her another feed to see if she settles. Keep this interaction very calm with no nappy change or stimulation and limit burping to 5 minutes. She should settle quickly if she needs the feed. If she doesn't settle and appears to be more restless, you have most likely over-fed her, causing her to feel uncomfortable.

> **SLEEP SECRET**
> Milk is still the only appropriate source of nutrition for your baby at this age. Do not be tempted to introduce solids at all at this stage.

GETTING IT RIGHT: SETTING THE STAGE

The environment in which your baby sleeps is very important to ensure that he is not over-stimulated. Sensory overload, which can cause over-tiredness, may lead to sleeping difficulties.

The sleep zone

If you have not encouraged a consistent sleep zone for your baby yet, now is the time to do so (see Chapter 3). From four months of age, your baby will begin to develop expectations and associations related to where and how she goes to sleep.

- Move your baby to her long-term sleep space – that is her own cot in your or her own room by four months of age.
- If your life is very busy and you and your baby are rarely at home, try to ensure that she goes to bed in her sleep zone for the night sleep and at least one day-sleep.
- If your baby consistently goes to sleep out of her sleep space (by being in the car or her pram) she will come to expect this as her sleep zone, and will resist going to bed in her sleep space at home.

Many parents find it hard at this stage to get their babies to sleep during the day. Look out for the following issues and work with them to get your baby to sleep more regularly during the day, which will undoubtedly help her to sleep better at night.

Introduce a sleep soother

Now is the time to ensure that the sensory input your baby your baby associates with sleep can be used independently eventually, such as a thumb, dummy or sleep soother (blanket or toy). Introduce this consistently at sleep time and whenever she is miserable. Read Chapter 7 for ways to implement this successfully

Help your baby to sleep regularly during the day

Implement these measures to help your baby sleep during the day. This will improve night sleeping.

AVOID SENSORY OVERLOAD AND OVER TIREDNESS

If your baby is over-stimulated between sleeps (even if you are watching her awake times), she will battle to switch off and fall asleep when you put her down during the day. At this age your baby is more alert than she used to be and she is taking in so much stimulation from the world around her.

- **Look out for her signals** that will tell you that she is getting overloaded such as becoming irritable, looking away from you and hiccups (see page 25).
- **Limit her *awake* time** to an age-appropriate time (see page 61). A two-month-old baby can manage with 60 minutes of awake time, extending it to 90 minutes by the time she is four months.
- **Use sense-able sensory steps:** Implement at least 10 minutes of calming input to help her to become sleepy. Try these sensory steps:
  - *Touch* Keep your baby swaddled in a stretchy, 100% cotton blanket for all day and night sleeps, and begin to encourage the use of a sleep soother or blanky at sleep time from the age of three months.
  - *Visual* Dim her room and cover the front of the pram to block out bright light at sleep times.

- **Sound** Use white noise at sleep time to help her settle and sleep deeper and longer.
- **Movement** Rock your baby or push her in a pram to settle her if she is fractious and is fighting sleep. Use a sling or a baby hammock to keep your baby close to you to help her to become drowsy.
- **Smells and taste** The taste of milk or smelling a familiar fragrance (such as yourself) is calming and helps to induce sleep

Establish a flexible day routine

If your baby is over tired, over-stimulated and struggling to sleep during the day, chances of her being in a day routine are slim. Starting to implement a flexible day routine will go a long way towards establishing healthy sleep habits that are appropriate for her age.

- Depending on the length of her sleeps, your baby will be having about four sleeps during the day (fewer if she sleeps for long periods of time). Remember to act on her signals and watch her awake times.
- You will notice a pattern emerging where at certain times of the day predictable events such as a sleep occur. Encourage this pattern by being consistent (same place, same time) and repeating it each day.
- Try to have a lie down when your baby is sleeping for at least one of her day sleeps.

Help your baby to link sleep cycles

Many babies do not link sleep cycles at this age and so each day sleep may only be 45 minutes long. This is quite normal, so don't worry if this is the case. But as she gets older, she will start to link her sleep cycles and begin to have longer day sleeps.

If you are lucky, and your baby **has** begun to link sleep cycles (closer to four months of age), she may have one or two long sleeps in the day lasting approximately one and a half hours. (Remember to wake your baby up during the day to feed if she has been sleeping for longer than four hours.) Try this technique to encourage your baby to link sleep cycles or if your baby is a 'cat napper':

- Listen for a few minutes when your baby wakes to see if she resettles herself with self-calming measures such as sucking her thumb or bringing her hands together.
- If she does not succeed and remains restless, respond by quietly and calmly re-swaddling her, encouraging hand to mouth activity, and pat her back to sleep.
- Keep trying for about 2-3 minutes, but if it does not work, accept the sleep is over and start watching her awake time again.
- You might find that the next period of **awake time** is slightly shorter than usual; be guided by her signals and put her back to sleep when she is ready.

> SLEEP SECRET
> Every baby is an individual and will settle into a routine at her own pace. One baby settles into a flexible routine almost from day one, another shows no pattern until later, and another may rigidly depend on routines and be thrown if anything unpredictable happens in her day. Do not compare your baby's routine with others'.

GETTING IT RIGHT AT BEDTIME

By now you know the importance of a regular day-sleep routine, but a regular bedtime routine is just as important. Bedtime is often the period of time when your baby is at her most unsettled, but if there is no pattern to your baby's bedtime rituals, such as a quiet bath, followed by the last feed of the day in her calm sleep zone, she will not begin to recognize the necessary sensory cues that prompt sleep.

A simple bedtime routine to ease her into sleep quicker

From this age, introduce a consistent time for bed with a predictable routine leading up to bedtime. Between 6 pm and 7 pm is an appropriate time for bed. Remember that this time will depend on when she awoke from her last afternoon sleep. Occasionally, you might need to push a slightly longer awake time in the late afternoon to coincide with your bedtime routine. Most babies can handle this if they are good sleepers, but if your baby is particularly unsettled at this time and bath time is a nightmare rather than a pleasurable time, rather let her have a short 'cat nap' for 45 minutes, wake her up and start your bedtime routine a bit later.

- Start the evening routine with a soothing warm bath followed by a calming massage (if your baby is still unsettled in the evenings, rather massage in the morning, as it may over stimulate her at this time). Keep bath time quiet and calm.
- After her bath wrap her in a warmed towel, take her into her sleep zone and dress her in cotton night clothes. Swaddle her, keeping all interactions in the room calming with limited handling and stimulation.
- Dim the lights, and feed your baby the last feed of the day in the dark. Keep her in your arms for this feed, so that she does not associate her bed with food. Take care not to over-stimulate her when burping her, and hold and rock her (if necessary) to make her drowsy. Take your time with this; it may take a while. Enjoy this special time with your baby.
- When your baby is relaxed and drowsy, but **not asleep** put her gently into her bed (not head first).

IF SHE WON'T SETTLE (FOR BOTH DAY AND NIGHT SLEEPS)

Often this period is marked with unsettledness after being put down to sleep. Try these simple strategies:

- Stay calm and place your hand gently anywhere on your baby and rhythmically pat her to sleep.
- Encourage non-nutritive sucking by letting her suck on your finger, a dummy, or her thumb or hand. Say 'shshsh' in a quiet tone of voice.

- If your baby continues to fuss and cry persist with this muted input for **5 minutes.** It is tempting to resort to erratic interventions such as lifting, patting, burping, nappy checks or feeding which may over-stimulate her.
- If she continues to cry, pick her up gently and re-swaddle her. You may need to hold her close and rock her gently and encourage non-nutritive sucking at this point to get her to stop crying and become drowsy again.
- If it is in the evening, offer her a top-up feed in case she is hungry.
- When she is relaxed and drowsy, put her into her bed.
- If she starts to niggle once again, sit with your hand on her, saying 'shshsh' for 5 minutes. If she begins to really cry pick her up, keep her swaddled, and if you have a sling or a pouch use it to keep her close to you. Walk with her and rock her until she is calm again, and put her into her bed.
- If she remains unsettled, repeat the procedure, but if a period of 15-20 minutes has passed, and she is not yet asleep then pick her up and walk with her and rock her until she is asleep.
- Once she is asleep, put her into her bed (not head first – you guessed it!).

SLEEP SECRET
A sling creates a womb space with calming sensory input of warmth, movement and deep touch pressure.

GETTING IT RIGHT AT NIGHT

To keep your baby on the path towards healthy sleep habits at night, follow these age appropriate guidelines:

- Don't wake your baby to feed her at night. Follow her natural sleep rhythm, which is to have a long period of sleep in the first part of the night. Waking your baby to feed her at 10 pm to avoid the 2 am feed rarely works. The establishment of good sleep cycles is disrupted by this forced waking. Your baby will probably feed very poorly as she is most likely not hungry enough to feed, and is very sleepy at this point. This may cause her to wake from hunger later, as she did not feed well enough at 10 pm. If you have woken your baby sufficiently to ensure she **does** feed well, she will most likely become wide awake and will not re-settle easily. This will obviously lead to further sleep disruptions.
- By now your baby may have stopped passing stools at every feed. If your baby's nappy is wet but clean do not change it at night so that night feeds are handled with the minimum of fuss.
- Your baby may start to sleep through the night on occasion. Do not expect her to consistently sleep through the night at this age, but rather accept that you may still have a few more nights of waking at least once to feed your baby.

Undesirable sleep habits

Your young baby does not have the memory capacity to develop firmly entrenched habits at this stage, so you do not need to worry about spoiling her by letting her fall asleep with you. Aim for her to fall asleep independently as she gets closer to four months of age, by implementing some of the strategies we discussed in the first section of the book (see page 69-75), but if she remains irritable and needs to be assisted to sleep it is not a major concern at this age.

COMMON SLEEP ISSUES FROM SIX WEEKS TO FOUR MONTHS
Light sleeper

My baby is eight weeks old. When we put him down to sleep, he seems to be in a 'light sleep' for a long time and the slightest noise wakes him. He sometimes screams for no reason in his sleep, and wakes himself up. If we comfort him he falls back to sleep easily, but this can happen up to eight times a night. We are desperate for some unbroken sleep, even if it is only for a few hours at a time.

Sleep solution: Take your little one for a full medical check up to exclude gastro-oesophageal reflux or pressure in his ears, which may be causing him to be such a restless sleeper. It may also be hunger that is keeping him awake, although it is unlikely as you are able to comfort him without feeding him. All newborns spend half their sleep in the light sleep or REM (rapid eye movement) state. In this restless state they wake easily and are sensitive to any stimulation in their environment, especially noise. A sleep cycle for young babies is 45 minutes so it is normal for your eight-week-old to only sleep for this long, especially during the day. Soon he will start linking sleep cycles (as he gets closer to four months of age) and sleep for a long stretch at least once a day. This long sleep usually occurs in the first half of the night, from bedtime to just after midnight.

To help him to start to sleep deeper, try **swaddling** him at sleep time in a stretchy, 100% cotton blanket. This will keep him snug and contained, and will prevent his arms from shooting out and waking him. This usually happens 15 minutes after he has gone to sleep. Be sure to keep his hands close to his face when you swaddle him so that he can suck on his fingers to self-calm. Persevere with swaddling even if your baby appears to hate it at first. Try using **white noise** in his sleep zone to block out sounds and to make him sleep a little deeper and for longer. If his restlessness persists, do discuss his nutrition with your clinic nurse, as hunger needs to be completely ruled out. Don't worry about spoiling him at this age; if he needs to be comforted back to sleep, do so.

Self-soothing difficulties

My little boy is now 11 weeks old and is showing signs of wanting to self-soothe and sucks ferociously on his hands. How can I swaddle him and encourage self-soothing at the same time? Also, is there any link between sucking their hands to self-soothe and ultimately becoming thumb-suckers?

Sleep solution: You are doing a wonderful job encouraging self-soothing strategies. Many babies younger than three months old struggle to keep their hands in their mouths for long enough to soothe themselves. After 12-14 weeks of age, they have more control of their little arms, and can keep their hands close to their mouth. This is when they start to derive some pleasure from sucking on their hands. (This is often mistaken for hunger or teething, of which is most likely neither!) Until your baby can keep his hands successfully in his mouth, use a dummy to keep him happy. It does not matter what your baby sucks on to self-soothe, as long as he has something.

If your baby keeps pushing his arms out of the swaddle blanket and does not seem to be interested in sucking on his hands for comfort, swaddle his hands together over his chest. He will still be calmed by the fact that his hands are together in the midline, and won't be able to extricate his arms from the blanket, which will keep him calm. Don't be tempted to swaddle his arms to his sides – he will not enjoy being restricted in this manner.

Some children who self-calm on their hands early on, do go on to become thumb suckers. There are pros and cons to dummies and thumbs but both play an important role in assisting your baby to self-calm. You may find yourself doing 'dummy patrol' for a while before he can independently use his dummy for comfort, but when he is old enough, you can easily teach him to do it himself (see page 71). The early days of dysregulation (where he can't soothe himself easily) pass quickly and before long his self-soothing strategies will become better developed.

Snack feeding day and night

My baby is three months old and is happy and content and growing well. However, she seems to be permanently hungry! She needs to feed frequently, but will never complete a feed and prefers to drink small amounts whenever she pleases. This occurs both during the day and at night. Surely she should be sleeping a bit more at this age?

Sleep solution: Provided she is gaining weight, try to break the cycle of snack-feeding in the following way.
- **To stretch during the day between feeds:** Begin with the **first** feed of the day. Let her have whatever quantity she wants in a period of no longer than 30 minutes.
- For the first day, do not give your baby milk if she cries or fusses less than three hours after the last feed. Offer her 30-50 ml of cooled, boiled water from a spoon or bottle. Encourage calming by hand-to-mouth or dummy sucking, and by gently rocking and soothing her. From the second day onwards, you may wish to increase this interval without feeding her milk to closer to four hours by implementing the same strategy. Not all babies are able to stretch to 4 hourly feeds.
- **To stretch at night between feeds:** After the last feed of the day at **bedtime**, stretch the interval to the next milk feed to as close to six hours as you can by offering her 30-50 ml of cooled, boiled water from a spoon or bottle. Encourage calming by hand-to-mouth or dummy sucking, and by gently rocking and soothing her. After this feed, do not stretch her for longer than four hours before offering her a feed.
- Continue with this cycle for at least 24 hours before you will see a change in her feeding pattern.
- Never leave her on her own to cry.
- Prepare yourself for a few rocky days and nights where it will seem she is permanently fussing. If you persevere it will pay off when she is able to stretch longer without needing to feed which will obviously mean more sleep for you!

Quick relief for tired parents – four to seven months

Your baby is full of delights and parenting is starting to seem worthwhile now that your baby is able to self-calm, and you are learning to read his signals better. But amongst all the joys of parenting, the reality has dawned – nothing will ever be the same again and that goes for sleep too. Even for parents whose baby is a good sleeper, some sleep cycles have changed and weekend lie-ins are a distant memory. What might happen at this stage, is that your baby who has slept well until now, suddenly begins to wake often at night. You've been sleep deprived for almost half a year now, so understandably might be feeling a bit desperate to get some much needed sleep

WHAT TO EXPECT IN TERMS OF SLEEP AT THIS STAGE

- If you are giving your baby a chance to find strategies to self calm (see Chapter 7), such as sucking on his hands or holding his hands together, he should be able to self-soothe back to sleep if he stirs at night and is not hungry.
- Most babies who self-soothe usually sleep through the night (10 hour stretch) by four to five months of age (provided hunger is not an issue). If you are getting your baby down to bed at night by 6 or 7 pm he should sleep until between 4 and 6 am before needing a feed. For some, 4 am might still seem like a night feed, but hang in there, it will get later!
- During the day your baby should be having three or four naps and a clear pattern to his day-sleeps will start to emerge.
- Sleep disruptions may arise at this stage, usually owing to changing nutritional needs.
- This is the time that bad habits can become entrenched. Your baby's memory begins to develop, causing sleep expectations to become an issue. Your baby will have certain expectations around sleep, such as the place and the manner in which he goes to sleep. Should he wake in the night, instead of being able to self calm, he will expect the same scenario to be re-enacted for him (such as being rocked or fed back to sleep).

GETTING IT RIGHT: THE BASICS

If your baby generally resists going to sleep at his day sleeps, battles to fall asleep at night or is waking more than once a night, you need to address the following issues, and get some sleep strategies in place right away. These strategies will help you to deal with the problem at hand, so that you can support sleep and teach your baby how to self-calm.

Rule out illness

If your baby is unusually irritable and not feeding, read Chapter 5 carefully or visit your doctor to be sure that your baby is not ill.

Rule out other health issues

Some babies teethe towards the end of this stage and a few nights of disruption must be expected. Read Chapter 5 for ideas on teething management and to exclude other issues which may be causing your baby to be very restless.

Your baby's nutritional needs

If your baby is still unsettled and not sleeping you will want to be sure he is not hungry. This is a common age when changing nutritional needs play havoc with sleep

Between four and six months of age, your baby's nutritional needs will change and where milk met all his caloric needs before, he may now need a bit more to settle his hunger. You will know its time to introduce solids when:
- Your baby is older than four months
- He has stopped growing despite drinking milk frequently
- He can no longer stretch 3½ to 4 hourly between day milk feeds
- He has begun waking earlier and earlier in the morning or for his night feed and is no longer able to stretch without a feed for any length of time at night
- He weighs in the region of 7 kg
- He sits supported in a chair and holds his head up well
- He is very interested in your food and reaches for a spoon.

IMPORTANT NOTE	The World Health Organisation (WHO) recommends exclusive breast feeding for at least six months if possible, so if you can manage with night feeds until your baby is six months old, (provided he is growing), don't rush into solids if you don't want to, especially if you have been advised to wait or if there are serious allergies in your family.

Do bear in mind that introducing solids does not magically 'make' babies sleep through the night, but as solids do sustain your baby's nutritional needs you will notice an improvement in his sleep, after a few weeks of incrementally introducing them. For full details and a schedule on introducing solids see Chapter 4 page 44).

After the age of six months, your baby's nutritional needs will change once more. This is when solid food **must** be introduced if you have not done so already.
- If you are bottle feeding, it is important to change your baby's milk to a more age-appropriate one.

- You will need to add sufficient protein into his solid diet, as this is very important from this age. See Chapter 4, page 46 for ideas.
- Ask your pharmacist or clinic nurse to prescribe an iron supplement for your baby.

GETTING IT RIGHT: SETTING THE STAGE

A common cause of night wakings at this stage is over-tiredness and over-stimulation. Creating the right circumstances to keep your baby calm will assist you in settling him at sleep times.

The sleep zone

The environment in which your baby sleeps is very important to ensure that he is not over-stimulated. Sensory overload that can cause over-tiredness may lead to sleeping difficulties.

- At this stage your baby forms expectations regarding where he goes to sleep. It is important to create a consistent sleep zone for him.
- By now your baby should be in his long-term sleep space, that is a cot in his own nursery or your room. Many babies sleep worse in their parent's bed as they are woken by sounds and movements when they are in a light sleep state.
- Even if your life is very busy you need to ensure that your baby goes to bed in his sleep zone for the night sleep and at least one day-sleep, preferably his longest sleep of the day.
- As your baby is so alert, a calming sleep zone takes on greater significance. Be sure to read Chapter 3 for ideas to create a calm sleep zone.

Introduce a sleep soother

Make sure the sensory input your baby associates with sleep can eventually be used independently. If you have not done so already, now is the time to introduce a sleep soother such as a blanket or soft toy. Whenever your baby cries when he is awake, whether it is for discomfort, tiredness or just for a cuddle, pick up the *sleep soother* and put it on your shoulder and then cuddle your baby against the **soother** on your shoulder. Before long your baby will attach to this security object (see Chapter 7). If your baby enjoys sucking his thumb or dummy, encourage him to do so.

Help your baby to sleep regularly during the day

Many parents report finding it hard to get their babies to sleep during the day. If your baby is not sleeping during the day, he will probably fight sleep in the evening and wake more often at night.

Avoid sensory overload and over tiredness

A common reason for sleep disturbances at this stage is over-tiredness and over-stimulation due to sensory overload. From the age of four months old, your baby is so much more alert than he used to be and he is taking in a lot of stimulation from the world around him.

- **Look out for his signals** that will tell you that he is getting overloaded such as becoming irritable, looking away or busy body movements (see page 61).
- **Limit his *awake* time** to an age-appropriate time (see page 25). A four-month-old baby can manage with one and a half hours (90 min) of awake time, and by the time your baby is 7 months old, he will manage to be awake for 2-2½ hours before he will need another sleep.
- **Use sense-able sensory steps:** Help him to become sleepy by spending at least 10 minutes calming him. Try these sensory steps:
  - *Touch* Although at this age he may prefer his arms not to be swaddled it is still important to wrap him under his arms in a blanket for all day and night sleeps. Be sure to encourage the use of his sleep soother or blanky at all sleep times.
  - *Visual* Dim his room at sleep times or cover the front of the pram to block out bright lights to create a calming sleep zone.
  - *Sounds* White noise is very effective in blocking out extraneous world sounds that could wake your alert baby. He will settle easier and sleep deeper and longer.
  - *Movement* Movement is still soothing before sleeps. Rock your baby in your arms to settle him into a drowsy state before sleep.
  - *Smells and taste* The familiar taste of milk, smells of mom and sleep space are calming and help to induce sleep.

Implement a day routine

As your baby gets older you can begin to guide him into a healthy day routine. Encouraging him to sleep regularly will help to prevent over-tiredness and over-stimulation.

- Watch the length of time he spends awake between sleeps and act on his signals when he is tired. If you do this your baby will be having in the region of three to four sleeps during the day (fewer if he sleeps for a long period of time).
- When your baby's sleeps become predictable encourage the routine by repeating it each day.
- Rest when your baby sleeps, especially if your nights are disturbed.

Help your baby to link sleep cycles

During this stage most babies begin to link sleep cycles during day. But if your baby is still only sleeping for 45 minute stretches, try these techniques to encourage him to link sleep cycles and have longer day sleeps:

- Listen for a few minutes when your baby wakes to see if he re-settles himself with self-calming measures such as sucking his thumb or bringing his hands together.

- If he does not succeed and remains restless, wait for two to five minutes before responding to him calmly and quietly.
- Rewrap him and encourage him to suck on his hands or dummy and use his sleep soother, change his position, and pat him back to sleep.
- Keep trying for about 2-3 minutes, but if it does not work, accept the sleep is over and start watching his awake time again.
- You might find that the next period of *awake time* is slightly shorter than usual, be guided by his signals and put him back to sleep when he is ready.

GETTING IT RIGHT AT BEDTIME

If you instil a pattern to your baby's bedtime ritual he will begin to recognize his sleep cues to begin to prepare for sleep. From this age, start to introduce a consistent bedtime (between 6 and 7 pm) with a predictable routine leading up to bedtime.

- Twice in the afternoon, for at least 5 minutes at a time, give your baby some movement input by rocking him in a hammock or baby swing. (You can do it for longer if your baby tolerates the movement well.)
- In the early evening, keep stimulation to a minimum and avoid rough play or intense movement activities. Dads – be warned!
- One hour before bedtime, start a calming bath-time with lavender fragranced products, dim lights, reduce interactions and noise.
- When you take him out of the bath, wrap him snugly in a warmed towel and handle him firmly and confidently, taking him into his sleep zone. Dress him in warm, cotton night clothes, and keep all interactions in the room calming with limited handling and stimulation.
- Wrap your baby in a soft blanket and give him his sleep soother.
- Dim the lights, and feed your baby the last feed of the day in the dark. Keep him in your arms for this feed, so that he does not associate his bed with food. Take care not to over-stimulate him when burping him, and hold and rock him (if necessary) to make him drowsy. Take your time with this, it may take a while. Enjoy this special time with your baby.
- When your baby is relaxed and drowsy, but **not asleep** put him gently into his bed (not head first) and leave the room.

If he won't settle (for both day and night sleeps)

If your baby continues to fight day sleeps, battle at bedtime and wake more than once at night, you may now need to help your baby learn to self-calm to settle himself to sleep. Please note at this stage you are not sleep training or letting your baby 'cry it out'; you are rather teaching the skill of self-calming and supporting sleep.

- If your baby cries as you put him down, stay calm and place your hand gently anywhere on his body and rhythmically pat him to sleep.

> **SLEEP SECRET**
> If you have a busy toddler around, elicit help from a granny, neighbour or Dad to allow you to focus on getting your baby to sleep if he is difficult to settle in the evening.

- Encourage non-nutritive sucking by letting him suck on a dummy, or his thumb or hand. Say 'shshsh' in a quiet tone of voice.
- Continue gently patting him for 5 minutes, even if he is fussing and crying. Often babies settle quicker with this muted input rather than erratic interventions of lifting, patting, burping, nappy checks or feeding you may otherwise resort to which just further over-stimulates them.
- If he continues to cry, pick him up gently and rewrap him. Tuck his sleep soother into his body once more. You may need to hold him close and rock him gently and encourage non-nutritive sucking at this point to get him to stop crying and become drowsy again.
- If your baby is not on solid food, offer him a top-up feed in case he is hungry.
- When he is relaxed and drowsy, put him into his bed
- If he starts to niggle once again, sit with your hand on him, saying 'shshsh' for 5 minutes. Encourage the use of his sleep soother. If he begins to really cry pick him up, keep him wrapped, rock him gently and put him down drowsy again.
- If he remains unsettled after repeating the process, lift him again and soothe him until he is **very** drowsy before putting him down again.
- Keep repeating this process until your baby falls asleep.

GETTING IT RIGHT AT NIGHT

Until your baby is on solid food, he may need nutritional support at night. Follow these age appropriate guidelines to make your nights manageable.

- Don't wake your baby to feed him at night. Follow his natural sleep rhythm, which is to have a long period of sleep in the first part of the night. Waking your baby to feed him at 10 pm to avoid the 2 am feed can disrupt his natural sleep cycle.
- If you use a good quality disposable nappy, there should be no reason to change his nappy at night if it is not soiled. If he has passed a stool change the nappy with a minimum of fuss in a dimmed room at night.
- Once your baby is on solid food during the day, he should be able to last for at least eight hours without needing a feed.
- If you do have to feed him, do so quietly and with a minimum of fuss and put him back to bed. You should not need to wind your baby at this age.
- If he will not settle after this feed, sit with him in your arms until he is drowsy, then put him into his bed and with gentle pressure, place your hand on him until he is asleep (see above strategies).
- Your baby may gradually start to sleep through the night. Do not expect your baby to consistently sleep through overnight at this age, but rather accept that you may still have a few more nights of waking at least once a night to feed him.

UNDESIRABLE SLEEP HABITS

Habits, or sleep associations are not necessarily a bad thing *if* they are used independently by your baby. However, **undesirable sleep habits** may develop at this age if your baby has not yet learnt to effectively self-calm or use a sleep soother. If he is used to being assisted to sleep, and cannot achieve this independently; he will expect this same 'habit' to be re-enacted when he wakes in the night. Undesirable sleep habits to watch out for at this stage include:

- Rocking or walking your baby to sleep
- Feeding your baby to sleep
- Replacing the dummy repeatedly at night
- Developing a dependence on movement to fall asleep, such as the car, car seat or pram

It is easy to exacerbate a dependent sleep habit by responding too quickly to your baby's fussing, never allowing him some time to self-calm. Teach your baby to self-calm using a sleep soother by reading Chapter 7. If necessary, begin some sleep modification techniques in order to teach your baby how to fall asleep unassisted (see page 92).

COMMON SLEEP ISSUES FROM FOUR TO SEVEN MONTHS
Nutritional needs change

Until recently our six-and-a-half-month-old baby was sleeping until 4 am, drinking a bottle and then sleeping until 6:30 am. This changed this week. He has taken to waking up at 3 am for a bottle and then at 5 am. When he wakes up at 5 am he is not interested in going back to sleep. I give him a dummy but he is wide-awake. During the day he is awake for 2-hour periods, and has no trouble going to sleep for his day naps, or at bedtime when he is put to sleep in his cot every night at 7 pm in a happy awake state. He does have a security object which he enjoys.

Sleep solution: Waking any time from 4 am to 6 am to have a feed is normal for this age, so do continue to feed him if he wakes at that time. The fact that he is starting to wake earlier in the night could be because he is hungry. If he is drinking formula milk, make sure he has moved to one that is appropriate for his age. He is ready to eat solid food now, so if you have not yet started him on solids, please ask your clinic nurse for advice, or follow the plan from Chapter 4 of this book. If he is already on solids, you now need to introduce sufficient protein in his diet in the form of dairy, meat, poultry and beans (see page 46 for ideas). It is also a good idea to start him on an iron supplement in case he is anaemic. Regarding the early morning waking; you may need to accept that for now your day starts at 5 am and enjoy this special time with your baby – before you know it, he'll be a teenager and you won't be able to get him out of bed in the morning!

Over stimulation wreaks havoc with sleep

I have a beautiful daughter who is five months old. I live with my fiancé and his parents, as we do not have our own home. The problem is that my baby never has a chance to sleep properly during the day as my father-in-law is always around and wanting to play with her whenever she is awake. He stimulates her so much in the evenings that she becomes over-tired and miserable. I am struggling to get him to understand that she needs quiet time before bed as I am left with a screaming baby who will not go to sleep. My fiancé is no real help as he says that he can't help her when she is crying.

Sleep solution: It sounds like your little one is simply overtired! As she is only five months old, her time spent awake in between naps during the day should be no longer than 1½ - 2 hours.

It is very important not to over-stimulate her, especially close to sleep time, as this will make her unable to self-soothe and settle down to sleep. If she is over-tired, she will cry and scream and she will need to be rocked and held to be quiet and stay calm. This may take a long time, and no wonder you are feeling tired, exhausted and frustrated! It is important to try to implement a day routine by watching her awake time and to allow her to go to sleep whilst she is still 'happily awake' – not when she is miserable and overtired. Bedtime should be between 6 and 7 pm. Once your father in law sees that a routine and controlled stimulation (in other words, stimulation at an appropriate time, not when she is tired) is what your daughter needs, he may adapt more easily to your wishes. Try to include your fiancé more in your daughter's care-giving – perhaps he is afraid of her when she is crying uncontrollably, and this is why he appears to be disinterested in helping you. Once your daughter is happier and calmer as she gets more sleep and is not as tired and overloaded as she is now, your fiance will probably take a more active role in her care-giving.

Hungry baby

My baby is four months old now and is breastfed, except for a single formula bottle feed, which she has at daycare at about 2:30 pm. She generally goes three hours between feeds, as she gets hungry and very cranky if we try stretching her between feeds. She has slept beautifully in a routine since she was about eight days old, and goes to bed at approximately 6:30 at night. She used to sleep all the way through until 6 am, then the onset of summer turned it into 5 am, and now it's closer 4 am or even, like this morning, 3:30 am! She actually wakes us up with her babbling and crowing, which goes on for about 5 to 10 minutes, after which she gets bored, and starts crying. I then feed her and put her to bed (with some difficulty sometimes) until about 5:30 am when she wakes us in the same way. People are saying she's hungry – but she never appears hungry otherwise – what do you think is happening?

Sleep solution: At your baby's age and without solid food in her diet, it is quite appropriate for her to be requesting a feed at night and so you are doing the right thing by breastfeeding her at night. When she wakes, listen to her 'babbling and crowing' and only respond once she is crying – this will give her the chance to resettle to sleep if she is able to. Encourage the use of a sleep soother or blanky and always have it available to her should she need comfort. Put her in a special night nappy at bedtime, as she may be waking because she is wet and uncomfortable. If you do have to feed her, keep it as business-like as possible – no lights on, no nappy change and no chatting. Put her straight down after the feed and she will be more likely to go back to sleep with ease.

If she starts consistently waking earlier and earlier, then introducing solids may be on the cards, so do ask your clinic sister for advice or follow the guidelines as laid out in Chapter 4 of this book. As far as her sensory world goes – keep her swaddled, and her environment supportive of sleep. Invest in a block-out blind, or tuck a black refuse bag into her window to keep her room dark for as long as possible so that the morning light doesn't wake her. Accept the fact that she may be up for the day at 5 am. Don't forget to put her back to sleep by 6.30 am again so that she does not start off her day over-tired.

Quick relief for tired parents – seven to 12 months

Your busy and most likely mobile baby has you running in circles around her all of her waking hours. Whilst your baby may be enjoying her newfound freedom, remember that babies at this age have no understanding of danger and your job is as much security officer as nurturer at this stage. It's an exhausting task, made worse if you are not getting a full night's sleep. If you are reading this, chances are that you are not! Read on for some useful sleep strategies.

WHAT TO EXPECT IN TERMS OF SLEEP AT THIS STAGE

- If you are giving your baby a chance to find strategies to self calm (see Chapter 7), such as sucking her thumb, or reaching for a sleep object such as a dummy or a blanket, she should be able to self-soothe back to sleep if she stirs at night and is not hungry.
- Most babies who have achieved the art of self-soothing, sleep through the night, as no nutrition is required in the form of night feeds at this age. You can expect your baby to be hungry if it is 10-12 hours since her last feed.
- Bedtime should be between 6 and 7 pm and your baby will wake for the day between 5 and 7 am
- If you are lucky, your baby may doze off after her first early morning feed and wake for the day an hour or so later
- During the day your baby should be having two to three naps and a clear pattern to her day routine should be in place.
- Sleep disruptions are common at this stage, usually owing to changing nutritional needs, separation or entrenched bad habits.

GETTING IT RIGHT: THE BASICS

If your baby generally resists going to sleep for day sleeps, battles to fall asleep at night, or is waking during the night, you need to address the following issues, and get some sleep strategies into place right away.

Rule out illness

You know your baby's temperament by now. If she becomes unusually restless at night or irritable during the day, consult your doctor and read Chapter 5 carefully to be sure that illness is not the cause of night wakings.

Rule out other health issues

Your baby will be in the throes of teething during this stage. Read Chapter 5 carefully to guide you in excluding issues such as teething and iron deficiency.

Your baby's nutritional needs

Milk alone is not sufficient for your baby at this age. If your baby is still waking frequently to drink during the night, it is important that you ensure that her nutrition is adequate before you can implement any sleep coaching strategies

- If you have not yet started your baby on solid food, it is essential that you do so now.
  - If you are bottle feeding, ensure that her formula is one that is appropriate for her age.
  - Milk feeds can be offered three times a day (on waking in the morning, after lunch and again at bedtime)
  - She should be eating solid food three times a day (breakfast, lunch and dinner), with a small snack mid-morning, and mid-afternoon
- It is important to introduce protein into her diet. She needs protein for healthy growth and development. Protein is an important source of necessary essential amino acids, which are the building blocks of brain development. These proteins include dairy, poultry, meat and beans, and should be included into each meal (for more ideas see page 46).
  - If your baby is a fussy eater or you are concerned that her protein intake is insufficient, consider adding a protein supplement into her milk at bedtime. Ask your pharmacist or clinic nurse to recommend a supplement that is appropriate for your baby.

GETTING IT RIGHT: SETTING THE STAGE

Your baby is susceptible to over-stimulation that can affect her sleep. Follow these guidelines to be sure she is primed for healthy sleep habits.

CAUTION

If you have a family history of allergies or your baby shows signs of allergies hold off on certain proteins such as nuts, dairy, fish, soy and eggs until after one year of age.

The sleep zone

The environment in which your baby sleeps should support sleep and ensure that she is not over-stimulated resulting in over-tiredness and sleeping difficulties (see Chapter 3).

- At this age, your baby has already developed expectations and associations related to where and how she goes to sleep, so if you haven't moved her to her long-term sleep space, now is the time to do so.
- If her room is close to yours, stop using the baby monitor (if you have been using one). You will hear her if she needs you and you may be over reacting to noises when she is sorting herself out.
- If your life is very busy and you and your baby are rarely at home, try to ensure

that she goes to bed in her sleep zone for the night sleep and at least one day sleep, preferably her longest sleep of the day.

- If your baby constantly goes to sleep out of her sleep space (in the car or her pram) she will come to expect this as her sleep zone, and will resist going to bed in her sleep space at home. Bear in mind that it gets harder to change sleep zones as your baby gets older.

Deal with separation issues

This is the classic age for separation anxiety and you may find your baby needs to be sure that you still exist, especially at night! If this is the case, play hide and seek and peek-a-boo during the day. Be sure to read Chapter 8 for a full discussion on dealing with separation anxiety if you feel this is the root of the sleep problems. Remember to always say goodbye and hello happily to avoid creating anxiety around separation.

Introduce a sleep soother

If you have not done so already, introduce a sleep soother such as a blanket, soft toy, or a dummy. If your baby enjoys sucking her thumb, encourage her to do so. She will be able to associate this sensory input with sleep. You can teach her to use these sleep soothers independently from now on. Introduce a sleep soother consistently at sleep time or whenever she is miserable.

If your baby has come to expect the dummy to be put into her mouth for her each time she wakes at night, it is time to teach her how to use it independently so you can stop being on 'dummy patrol' during the night. The dummy is a great sleep tool for her to use effectively to help her self-soothe during the night. See Chapter 7 for hints and tips on teaching your baby to use her dummy independently.

Movement stimulation

Twice in the afternoon, for at least 5 minutes at a time, give your baby some intense movement input by rocking her in a hammock or swinging her in a baby swing. (You can do it for longer if your baby tolerates the movement well.)

Help your baby to sleep regularly during the day

Your baby's busy world around her still has the potential to easily overwhelm her. If she is over-stimulated she will become over-tired very quickly, and will be grumpy and difficult, especially around sleep time.

AVOID SENSORY OVERLOAD AND OVER TIREDNESS

A common reason for sleep disturbances at this stage is over-tiredness and over-stimulation due to sensory overload. Bedtimes may become difficult owing to lack of sleep during the day, and your baby will most likely wake frequently during the night. If your baby is mobile, she is no doubt very busy, so she will be taking in an enormous amount of stimulation from her world.

- Look out for her signals that will tell you that she is becoming overloaded such as becoming irritable, rubbing her eyes and ears or refusing food (see page 61).
- Limit her *awake* time to approximately 2½ hours (see page 25).
- Try to schedule stimulation classes and outings around her sleeps.
- At sleep time use sensory calming strategies to help her become sleepy (see page 38).

IMPLEMENT A DAY ROUTINE

By this age you can expect your baby to be establishing a nice routine.
- Depending on the length of her sleeps, she will be having in the region of two to three sleeps during the day (only two if she sleeps for a long period of time). Remember to act on her signals, and to watch her *awake* time. One of her day sleeps is likely to be longer than 45 minutes – this usually occurs towards late morning, which eventually will become her one sleep of the day in her toddler years.
- When she is about nine months of age, one of her sleeps may disappear, and she will most likely only need two sleeps during the day. (See Cusp ages, page 65.)
- If you are still struggling to instil a routine, watch for a pattern to emerge when specific events such as a feed or sleep occur. Encourage this pattern by being consistent (same place, same time) and repeating it each day.
- Always wake your baby if she is sleeping after 4.30 in the afternoon.
- If your baby is still waking at night, try to have a lie down at some point in the day – this will ensure you are well rested to handle the night.

HELP YOUR BABY TO LINK SLEEP CYCLES

Some babies do not link sleep cycles at this age and so each day sleep may only be 45 minutes long. But as she gets older, she will be able to link her sleep cycles and begin to have longer day sleeps. If your baby consistently wakes after 45 minutes for all day sleeps:
- Listen for a few minutes to see if she re-settles herself with self-calming measures such as sucking her thumb or reaching for her sleep soother.
- If she does not succeed and remains restless, wait for 2-5 minutes before responding to her calmly and quietly. If she is crying respond immediately.
- Re-wrap her (if she still enjoys this), encourage hand to mouth activity and her sleep soother, change her position, and pat her back to sleep.
- Keep trying for about 2-3 minutes, but if it does not work, accept the sleep is over and start watching her awake time again.
- You might find that the next period of *awake time* is slightly shorter than usual; be guided by her signals and put her back to sleep when she is ready.

GETTING IT RIGHT AT BEDTIME

The bedtime routine you use must be calming and consistent. It is then a cue for the brain to start shifting down into the drowsy state for bedtime.

- From this age, start to introduce a predictable routine leading up to bedtime which is between 6 and 7 pm. Remember that the time for bed is related to the time she woke from her afternoon sleep.
- Occasionally, you might need to push a slightly longer awake time in the late afternoon to coincide with your bedtime routine. Most babies can handle this if they are good sleepers, but if your baby is particularly unsettled at this time and bath time is a nightmare rather than a pleasurable time, rather let her have a short 'cat nap' for 30 minutes, wake her up and start your bedtime routine a bit later.
- In the early evening, your young baby is very susceptible to sensory overload and melt down. This is especially true if she is at a day sleep cusp age and has dropped her afternoon nap. Be sure to keep stimulation to a minimum and avoid rough play or exciting activities.
- Start the evening routine with a soothing warm bath followed by a calming massage. Keep bath time quiet and calm.
- When you take her out of the bath, wrap her snugly in a warmed towel and handle her firmly and confidently. Take her into her sleep zone and dress her, and put her in a sleeping bag for the night if she has started to kick off her bedclothes and keep all interactions in the room calming with limited handling and stimulation.
- Rub a few drops of **Rescue Remedy** (available from your pharmacy) directly onto her wrist and temple pulse points and on the soles of her feet.
- Encourage the use of her sleep soother, dim the lights, and feed your baby the last feed of the day in the dark. Keep her in your arms for this feed, so that she does not associate her bed with food. Take care not to over stimulate her – just hold and rock her (if necessary) to make her drowsy. Take time, slow down and relish these quiet moments with your baby – they are few and far between.
- When your baby is relaxed and drowsy, but **not asleep** put her gently into her bed (not head first), kiss her goodnight and leave the room.

If she won't settle (both day and night sleeps)

At this age, so many babies are battling to fall asleep independently. If your baby is not settling at sleep times, and **you have followed all the steps so far,** it is now time to implement some healthier sleep habits. You are going to have to teach your baby to fall asleep independently without being rocked or held.

METHOD ONE: STAYING WITH YOUR BABY

If your baby begins to fuss as soon as you put her down or the second you leave the room, you may have to sit with her for a few nights until she gets used to self-calming. This will entail patting and soothing her for the first night, then gradually withdrawing your presence in the sleep zone over subsequent nights by simply sitting alongside her cot without talking to her. Do not look worried or concerned, rather just close your eyes. Give her her **sleep soother** and help her lie down if she stands but other than that, just sit with her. She may cry if she is expecting to be rocked to sleep but be consistently unwavering. Keep this up until she falls asleep. You will have to repeat this procedure when she wakes in the night. Over the period of a few nights, she will have learnt the art of self-soothing. If she can only fall asleep if she is feeding, adopt the strategy mentioned below (feeding to sleep habit).

METHOD TWO: LEAVING YOUR BABY FOR SHORT PERIODS OF TIME
If you feel short periods of separation from your baby whilst sleep coaching works better for you because you cannot bear the thought of sitting alongside your crying baby, this method is for you. When your baby begins to cry or fuss when you put her down, see if you can settle her with a soothing touch. If not, pick her up and calm her down. As soon as she is drowsy again, place her in her cot and leave the room. If she cries, wait outside the sleep zone for one minute, then go back to re-settle her once more, even if it means picking her up to calm her before trying again. Increase the time spent out of her sleep zone by one minute each time and keep doing this until you have reached a maximum of 6 minutes outside and keep it at this. Repeat this procedure each time she wakes in the night.

Both methods are discussed in depth in Chapter 9 of this book. Read both methods thoroughly and choose one that you think will work for you. Remember to be consistent once you have decided which method to implement, and stick to it for at least a week before changing.

GETTING IT RIGHT AT NIGHT

Undesirable sleep habits become entrenched so easily, especially if your baby has not yet learnt to self-calm effectively or use a sleep soother. If she is used to being assisted to sleep, and cannot achieve this independently, she will expect this same habit to be re-enacted when she wakes at night. The good news is that your baby is old enough now to learn new skills and break past habits. Some habits are hard to break and if your baby has been crying a lot, she may need to sip on some cooled boiled water to quench her thirst. Add some **Rescue Remedy** to the water to help calm her down. A drop of **Rescue Remedy** per kilogram of your baby's weight is a safe dosage to use. Be sure to meet your baby's needs during the day and give her lots of love and cuddles.

Breaking the feed-to-sleep habit

The comfort of sucking on the breast or bottle can lead to sleep problems if your baby has learnt to fall asleep only when sucking, whether this is when she goes to sleep or when she wakes at the night. You need to break this habit by not **feeding** her to sleep. If you have made sure your baby's diet is adequate for her age, she no longer needs nutritional support in the form of milk feeds during the night. A feed after 4 am may be appropriate if your baby has been asleep for

10 hours. Feed your baby milk at the appropriate times, and if it is close to sleep time, ensure that she has finished feeding before she falls asleep. The first step is to get her used to falling asleep **without feeding.** Follow these simple guidelines:

- When the feed is finished, or when she wakes in the night expecting a feed, pick her up and hold her close to you. Rock her gently and soothe her until she is asleep, no matter how much she protests (nor how long it takes).
- Remember to remain in the sleep zone with your baby and to keep the environment quiet and calm.
- When she is asleep, place her back in her cot. Should she wake, repeat the procedure until she is asleep.
- Bear in mind this may take a few days to perfect, so don't give up.
- When she is used to the fact that she is able to fall asleep without feeding, and is happy to fall asleep in your arms, move to the next step, which is to teach her to go to sleep independently in her bed. Begin to implement any one of the sleep modification strategies mentioned above.

Breaking the rock-to-sleep habit

Your baby is quite capable of self-calming by this age. If she will only fall asleep whilst being rocked in your arms, this may be a deeply entrenched sleep habit that, surprisingly, is not that hard to break once you have taught her to self-soothe.

Adopt either one of the sleep training strategies mentioned above to teach your baby how to effectively self-calm

Stopping the dummy patrol

Being woken countless times during the night to do dummy patrol is common at this stage of your child's life. The dummy is a great sleep soother if your baby can use it independently to self-calm when she wakes during the night. It is quite reasonable to teach your baby at this age to use her dummy on her own to effectively self-calm. Teach her how to use her dummy independently by following the simple steps in Chapter 7 (see page 71).

Breaking the car-sleep habit

In general, make sure your baby goes to sleep in her cot at this age for day sleeps as well as at night. If your baby has only ever associated sleep with the car, she will protest falling asleep in her cot in her sleep zone. To help her making the transition from falling asleep in the car to falling asleep in the cot, follow these steps:

- The first few days stop going out in the car at sleep times altogether and rather put her in her pram and rock her to sleep in her sleep zone. In this way, the movement is kept consistent but the sleep space changes.

- When she is at the stage of falling asleep happily in her pram, begin to rock the pram only until she is drowsy, then leave the pram still and let her fall asleep.
- Once she is falling asleep with no movement, put her straight into her cot at sleep time. Don't forget to always help her to get drowsy first. She may need some help in the form of patting for the first few days of being in her cot.

COMMON SLEEP ISSUES FROM SEVEN TO 12 MONTHS
Night feeds

My baby is eight months old and wakes up roughly every 2 hours. She is a very light sleeper and is woken up by the slightest sounds, like her dad's snoring. She sleeps in her pram next to my bed as I only have one bedroom in my house. Once she's up, she will only go back to sleep if I breastfeed her to sleep. I tried giving her water or juice to drink but she turns her head away and cries until she gets the breast.

Sleep solution: To be on the safe side, your doctor needs to rule out any medical problems that may be causing her to wake so frequently. Check with your clinic nurse that she is getting enough nutrition in the day, and then you will know for sure that she does not need feeding in the night. Night feeds for an eight-month-old baby are inappropriate and not necessary. Until **you** are ready to take the step of no longer offering her a feed when she wakes, no sleep training will work, and she will never learn how to self-soothe. Do not feed to settle her, no matter how much she is crying. Rather hold her, rock her (offer her sips of water if she has been crying for a long time and may be thirsty). It will take her a few nights to learn to fall asleep without a feed.

When she is falling back asleep in your arms (without a feed), start putting her in her pram when she is merely drowsy, but not asleep. Always pick her up and console her if she won't settle with a few pats and soothing words. Only put her back in her pram once she has stopped crying. If you want to change things, you have to follow through on this in a consistent manner. Try to focus on the positive benefits of teaching her to go to sleep on her own, rather than getting bogged down with your fatigue now.

Co-sleeping disrupting sleep

I have an 11-month-old daughter, Bella, who has developed sleep problems. In the first six months of her life, she slept in a cot next to our bed. She would always fall asleep with a bottle at 7 pm. When she woke up during the night, I would hold her and she would fall asleep again quickly. When she was six months old, I moved her into her own room. She still fell asleep with a bottle. When she woke up at night, it was not so easy to get her back to sleep, and for my own sanity I would put her in bed with me and she would then go to sleep. As a working mom, I need as much sleep as I can get! Recently, however, she does not want to go to sleep until past eight at night. She is so restless, that even when I put her in bed with me, I get little sleep.

Sleep solution: Before you begin with any form of sleep training, it is advisable to take Bella to the doctor to check she is 100 % well. If she is well and is getting appropriate nutrition during the day (check her diet out with your clinic nurse), you are going to have to implement some sleep coaching strategies to teach her how to fall asleep independently. Her expectations of assistance to fall back asleep in the night are quite reasonable considering the way she falls asleep at night. If she is reliant on a bottle in order to fall asleep at bedtime, she will be looking for help again when she wakes during the night. You are on the right track at least by not feeding her another bottle in the night, but you do need to teach her to fall back asleep independently. She is restless in your bed because **you** are most likely disturbing her! Try to take a few days leave from work while you are sleep coaching so that you can catch up on some much needed rest.

Separation anxiety

I had my baby at home for seven months and started working again a week ago, half days. She stays with my mother-in-law and seems very happy. The problem is just that all of a sudden she wakes up at about 3 am and seems happy and chatty and wants to sit up, and doesn't want to go to sleep again for about 2 hours. She never did this; she used to sleep through till about 6 am.

Sleep solution: It is a good idea to check with your clinic nurse that your baby's milk and solid food intake is adequate during the day. At this age, she should be expected to sleep from 6 pm to between 4 am or 6 am without waking for a feed. It is also important that you give her an iron supplement every day. She is most likely going through a patch of separation anxiety as you have started work. Spend good quality time with her when you are home and play separation games such as hide and seek and peek-a-boo. Always say goodbye to her when you leave and greet her happily when you return. If she wakes at night and talks to herself, give her some time to re-settle before you go in to her. If she begins to cry, go to her and comfort her, then put her in her preferred sleep position and help her find her sleep object (blanky or dummy or thumb), then leave the room. You may have to repeat this procedure a few times until she settles back to sleep. If her sleep space is close to yours, switch off your baby monitor if you are still using one. She may be enjoying the novelty of sitting, as this is a skill she has most likely just mastered. This is most likely a passing phase, so don't worry unduly.

Quick relief for tired parents – 12 to 18 months

Congratulations! You have survived the first year of parenthood. Your baby is a toddler now and while you are most likely loving this mobile and interesting stage of your baby's life, if you are not sleeping it can be very hard going at times. You are in good company though – half of all toddlers are still waking their parents at night. However, statistics provide you with little comfort at 2 am. It is time to get a good night's sleep.

WHAT TO EXPECT IN TERMS OF SLEEP AT THIS STAGE

- From a developmental perspective, it is completely reasonable to expect your toddler to sleep for a stretch of 11-12 hours– from 6 or 7 pm to between 5 and 7 am.
- At a year of age your toddler will be enjoying two good sleeps during the day, approximately 3½ hours apart. Soon after his first birthday, he will reach a stage when he can manage to be happily awake for longer periods. He may begin to fight day sleeps and you will need to adjust his day-sleep routine during this stage. (See cusp ages, page 65).
- Your toddler should have all the strategies in place to be able to self-soothe and no longer needs any nutritional support at night.
- However, your toddler may present with sleep issues now based on the fact that he is at a stage of development where he is able to assert himself and push any boundaries you may have in place, particularly around bedtime.
- Undesirable sleep habits that may have been formed in the first year of life are firmly entrenched by now.
- Toddlers are notoriously fussy eaters, and you may be concerned about his nutritional status as a cause of night wakings.

GETTING IT RIGHT: THE BASICS

If you are still dealing with sleep issues or they have raised their ugly head at this stage, you need to rule out the basics to establish the reason for sleep problems at this age before even thinking of sleep coaching:

Rule out illness

As your toddler learns to walk at this stage, he becomes increasingly curious and will explore places that harbour germs. For this reason, he may be more susceptible to illness. Read Chapter 5 carefully to be sure that your toddler is not ill.

Rule out other health issues

Your toddler will be cutting incisors and molars at this stage. Read Chapter 5 carefully to exclude issues such as teething or worms.

Your toddler's nutritional needs

Your toddler should be on a mixed and varied diet by now, and has the capacity to eat all the food you eat as a family, just not the inclination or the will.

- **Don't worry** if he appears to become a picky or poor eater. His growth rate slows down dramatically from one to two years of age, which will affect his appetite. It will surprise you how little food your toddler will thrive on.
- Try to stick to the principle of a **varied diet** that includes protein such as meat, poultry, dairy, beans, nuts and seeds; carbohydrates such as bread, cereal, rice, pasta and potato and fats such as avocado, cheese and butter, as well as a variety of fruit and vegetables. Offer him small and frequent meals. He will eat if he is hungry.
- Too much milk will **spoil his appetite** and, in fact, milk is no longer a primary source of nutrition at this age.
- Offer him **milk** (breast, toddler formula or full cream cow's milk) twice a day, once on waking, and again at bedtime in the evening. Don't be tempted to replace a meal with milk.
- If you are worried that your toddler is not growing, add a toddler protein **supplement**, or a specially fortified formula into his evening milk. This will ensure adequate growth and that he is not hungry during the night.
- A good **multivitamin** and **iron supplement** to ensure healthy growth and development is a good idea to give him at this age. Ask your clinic nurse or pharmacist to recommend one for you.
- Nutrition is seldom a cause of night waking at this age. If your child is healthy and thriving, but is a poor eater during the day, do not worry.
- Now that your toddler is exposed to all types of food, as far as possible avoid giving him anything to eat or drink that contains added sugar or caffeine.

GETTING IT RIGHT: SETTING THE STAGE

Your toddler's environment and the experiences in his day affect his sleep. Take note of these areas to be sure that he is primed for good sleep habits.

The sleep zone

A sleep zone is an excellent sleep cue. If used consistently it prepares your toddler for sleep as soon as he sees his cot and the darkened room.

- Your toddler must remain in his cot and **not** be moved to a bed at this age. As long as he is happy in his cot, and he is not climbing out (which is obviously a safety risk) leave him there for as long as you can.
- The environment your toddler sleeps in is very important to ensure that he is not over-stimulated. Keep this space calming (see page 38).

- If you have not encouraged a consistent sleep zone for your toddler yet, it is important that you do so now. At this age, he already has expectations and associations related to where and how he goes to sleep, and you can use them to your advantage.
- White noise such as a fan, humidifier or a white noise CD will filter household noise and help him to settle.
- Make sure the room is dark enough for sleep – use block-out lining for your curtaining (this is important to limit early morning wakings and to encourage good sleep during the day).
- At night keep the room dim and muted or use a night-light, so that your toddler is never left alone in the dark. His imagination is developing at this age, which might make him fearful of dark shadows.

Deal with separation issues

Separation anxiety can be an issue at this stage and you may find your toddler needs to be sure that you still exist, especially at night! If this is the case, play hide and seek during the day and remember to always say goodbye and hello happily to avoid creating anxiety around separation. Be sure to read Chapter 8 for a full discussion on dealing with separation anxiety if you feel this is the root of the sleep problems.

The value of a sleep soother

Sensory input should be used to help your toddler sleep. It is never too late to introduce a sleep soother such as a blanket or a soft toy. To do so, offer him the blanky consistently at sleep time or whenever he is miserable. He should be able to use a dummy to self-calm independently by now. If not, teach him how, following the strategies on page 71.

Movement stimulation

Make sure your toddler gets a lot of movement input and heavy muscle activity during the day. This stage is one in which the brain naturally seeks movement and deep pressure on the body. This stimulus is important for the development of gross motor-skills and is the reason your toddler is so busy. If your toddler has not had this heavy muscle activity in the day and rather spends his time watching TV or involved in primarily quiet or sedentary activities, he is more likely to wake at night. Switch the TV off 2 hours before your toddler's bedtime.

Help your toddler to sleep during the day

Your little toddler is most likely very mobile by now, and has a much greater capacity for stimulation and interactions. If your toddler is not sleeping during the day or is over-stimulated you will have bedtime battles and restless nights.

Avoid sensory overload and over tiredness

It is still important for you to watch that over-stimulation and over-tiredness are not causing your toddler's sleep problems.

- Watch for signals that he is getting overloaded, such as becoming irritable, refusing to co-operate, rubbing his eyes or refusing food (see page 61).
- Limit his *awake time* to 3½-4 hours (see Chapter 6 page 25) between naps during the day.
- Try to schedule stimulation classes and outings around his sleep times.
- At sleep time, help him to "switch off" by trying to do at least 10 minutes of calming **sensory experiences** to help him become sleepy.

Establish a day sleep routine

If your toddler is over-tired, over-stimulated, and struggling to sleep during the day, chances of him being in a day routine are slim. A healthy day routine will go a long way towards helping him establish healthy sleeping habits that are appropriate for his age.

- Depending on the length of his sleeps, your little toddler will be having one to two sleeps during the day. Remember to act on his signals, and to watch his *awake time* (3½-4 hours). For example, a one-year-old will manage to last for about 3 to 3½ hours before he needs a nap, whereas an 18-month-old toddler will be able to stay awake for 4 hours.
- As your toddler gets a little older, he will start to stretch his awake time during the day, and will want to go to sleep later. Follow his lead and move both day sleeps a little later.
- Close to 15 months of age, your baby hits the next **day sleep cusp age** when he actually still needs to sleep twice a day, but begins to resist one or both sleeps. Bedtime in the evening may also be affected. At this point, he will drop the earlier morning nap and will push through until a late morning or midday nap.
- At 10:30 am offer him a hearty, nutritional snack, such as an egg on toast or a sandwich and yoghurt, so if he sleeps through lunch it does not matter. Your goal is to aim for one long midday sleep.
- Do not wake your toddler from this sleep. If he wakes before 12:30 he will need a cat nap in the afternoon, from which you must wake him by 4:30 pm so that bedtime does not become too late.
- If he has this cat nap, bedtime will be closer to 7 pm. If he wakes after 12:30 pm and has no afternoon nap, you should then move bedtime earlier to 6 pm at the latest.

GETTING IT RIGHT AT BEDTIME

By now you know the importance of a regular day sleep routine, but a regular **bedtime routine** is just as important. Bedtime is often the period when your little toddler is at his most unsettled. If there is no pattern to his bedtime rituals such as a quiet bath, followed by the last feed of the day in a calm sleep zone, your little toddler will not begin to recognize the necessary sensory cues that prompt sleep. Follow a simple bedtime routine to ease him into sleep more quickly:

- Start to introduce a consistent time for bed with a predictable routine leading up to bedtime. Depending on the time of his afternoon nap an appropriate time for bed is between 6 and 7 pm.
- In the early evening, keep stimulation to a minimum and avoid rough play or intense movement activities. Dads – be warned!
- The evening routine begins with a warm soothing bath followed by a calming massage (if he lies still). Wrap your toddler snugly in a warmed towel after his bath.
- After the bath, take him into his sleep zone, dress him and keep all interactions in the room calming with limited handling and stimulation. Do not leave the bedroom; rather engage in 'floor time' activities such as reading or quietly playing with building blocks.

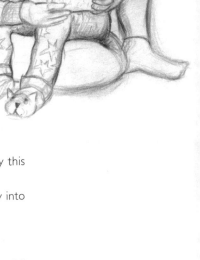

- Rub a few drops of **Rescue Remedy** (available from your pharmacy) directly onto his pulse points at his wrists and temples. If he will let you, rub some onto the soles of his feet.
- Dim the lights, encourage the use of his sleep soother and feed him the last feed of the day in the dark. Keep him in your arms for this feed, so that he does not associate his bed with food. Rock him (if necessary) to make him drowsy. Take your time with this, it may take a while. Enjoy this special time with your child.
- When your baby is relaxed and drowsy, but **not asleep** put him gently into his bed (not head first), kiss him goodnight and leave the room.

If he won't settle (both day and night sleeps)

If you have followed all the steps so far, but your baby is still not able to fall asleep without assistance, it is now time to implement some sleep modification techniques in the form of sleep coaching. There are two methods of handling this, the one method is to stay in the room with your toddler while he learns to self soothe, and the other method is to leave the room for short intervals of time, picking him up and comforting him each time you return. Let's tell you a little bit about each method.

METHOD ONE: STAYING WITH YOUR TODDLER

This sensible method works well if you feel happier staying with your toddler while he is learning to put himself to sleep. You simply stay with your toddler (even if he is crying) until he goes to sleep. With each subsequent night you distance yourself further away from his bed, but you remain in the room with him. All sleep coaching is hard work and may be very emotionally draining, so if you feel angry and frustrated when your toddler cries and feel that you might physically harm him, out of tiredness and frustration, then this is not the sleep modification method for you.

METHOD TWO: LEAVING YOUR BABY FOR SHORT PERIODS OF TIME

This method of sleep modification allows you to pick up your toddler when he is crying and to comfort him until he is calm, but it differs from the first method in that you actually leave the room for short periods of time from the beginning. Some parents may feel uncomfortable with separating from their toddlers, so method one is preferable for them. But for other parents, using short periods of separation from their toddler while sleep coaching works better as they find sitting alongside their crying toddler is difficult.

- Both methods are discussed in depth in Chapter 9 of this book. Read this chapter thoroughly and choose the method that you think will work for you. Remember to be consistent once you have decided which method to implement, and stick to it for at least a week before changing.
- Only sleep train if you are certain that all the basics have been ruled out as causes for night wakings and only embark on sleep training if you and your partner agree on the method.
- Some habits are hard to break and if your baby has been crying a lot, he may need to sip on some cooled boiled water to quench his thirst. Add some **rescue remedy** to the water to help calm him down. A drop of **Rescue Remedy** per kilogram of your child's weight is a safe dose.
- If your toddler is ill, all rules go out the window. This is a time to love and nurture him until he is well. If any bad habits become entrenched, simply deal with them when he is well again.
- Be sure to meet your child's needs during the day and give him lots of love and cuddles.

GETTING IT RIGHT AT NIGHT

Be sure your toddler has a transition object or **sleep soother**. A transition object is a tool your toddler can use as he makes the transition from dependence on you for comfort during sleep to complete independence.

Night feeds

Your young toddler does not need nutritional support at night at this age. Should he still be waking to feed at night, give him a chance to fall back to sleep on his own by waiting a few minutes before going into his room. If he continues to cry, go in to him and tell him that he must go to sleep and give him his sleep soother and a quick pat. This will most likely not satisfy him but you will begin to give him the message that night feeds are no longer an option. If he continues to cry, pick him up and comfort him, but do not feed him.

Hold and rock him until he is drowsy **no matter how long** it takes. Then lovingly put him back to bed. You may need to implement further sleep coaching strategies at this point. Refer to Chapter 9.

Baby in the bed

If your baby wakes frequently at night you will be exhausted. You may be tempted to take the path of least resistance and bring your baby into your bed so that you can carry on sleeping. When this becomes a habit you may realize that it is not what you would like to be doing every night. The simple solution is not to start. Should you be battling with this scenario, sleep coaching will be necessary.

If having your toddler sleep with you is not an issue for you and your partner, there is no reason to change. Bear in mind bringing your toddler into your bed at 5 am for a feed when he wakes is fine, as long as he goes back to sleep and does not disturb you. Many toddlers do come to mommy's bed in the early morning without having to do so in the middle of the night.

COMMON SLEEP ISSUES FROM 12 TO 18 MONTHS
Early mornings

I have a 15-month-old daughter who wakes every morning around 4.30 am for a bottle. How can we get her to sleep until at least 5.30 am?

Sleep solution: Toddlers are typically early morning risers, which can really be the bane of your life if you by nature are not an early riser. In the early hours of the morning, our environment and bodies cool down and we may wake up because of these lowered temperatures. Your toddler no doubt feels cold and uncomfortable owing to a wet nappy. First, try to prevent your toddler waking from cold by letting her sleep in a 100 % cotton sleeping bag, specifically designed for babies and toddlers. Also make sure her room is dark enough and that morning light is not waking her. Use block out lining for your curtaining or blinds. Increase the quantity of milk you are giving her at bedtime to be sure that it is not hunger that is waking her. If it is 5 am or later, offer her a feed, and with a bit of luck she will doze back to sleep. If she still continues to wake before 5 am and you have ensured that she is warm and not hungry, you may have to implement some sleep coaching strategies. Alternately, you can try to push her as close as you can to a goal of waking at 5.30 am by not giving her the bottle as soon as she wakes up at 4.30 am. The first morning, stretch it by 10 minutes, then increase it by 5 minutes each morning until she has to wait until 5.30 am for that first bottle. Some babies wake very early if bedtime is too late. So aim for a bedtime between 6 and 7:30 pm.

Habits

My baby is 13 months old. He wakes up hourly during the night and drinks up to six bottles per night. I took him to the paediatrician who checked him from head to toe and advised I should close his bedroom door at night and forget about him till morning. We started this on Monday night. He cried for 2 hours non-stop, slept for 40 minutes and started crying again. To stop the crying I had to give him a bottle of water. (I normally give him juice or milk.) It's not easy to let him cry without going into the room. Last night he woke three times, but would not go back to sleep unless I gave him the water bottle. Please advise if I should completely ignore him during the night and let him cry himself to sleep again, or can I give him water to replace the juice and only after that stop the bottle completely.

Sleep solution: Do not leave your little one to cry it out without you being with him. He does need to learn how to go back to sleep independently when he wakes in the night. If he is having six bottles of milk at night, he probably does not have a great appetite during the day. You need to stop all night feeds so that he gets his nutrition during the day. Make sure he eats properly during the day, plenty of fruit and vegetables and starch but also good protein, which is important for brain growth. It is also a good idea to give him a good iron supplement – ask your pharmacist for advice.

To break a habit you need to help your little boy establish better skills to help him fall asleep independently. This does not mean he must be left to cry. Firstly you have done the right thing by replacing the milk bottles with water. When you put him down at night, feed him his last milk bottle for the night, in your arms, not in his bed. Then put him down. If he fusses, sit with him and pat him and offer him his comfort object – something like a teddy or blanky that he can fall asleep with independently, without having to call you in the middle of the night. Each time he wakes at night, first offer him his comfort object, then sit with him and pat him or shshsh him. If he is very unsettled, offer him his water bottle. If he becomes hysterical and won't settle, pick him up and soothe him until he is asleep. When he is happy to go back to sleep at night without drinking anything (this may take a few nights), move to the next step which is to only hold him in your arms until he is drowsy, then put him into his bed to fall asleep on his own. See Chapter 9 for sleep coaching options to help you teach him to go to sleep on his own. It will take a few nights, but soon he will learn to self-soothe and to resettle himself.

Falling asleep in the car

My baby is 13 months old. Everything is going really well, except for her sleeping habits. Since she was a small baby, she would only ever fall asleep if she was pushed in a pram or if she fell asleep in the car. It never really worried me until now where we have reached a point where she will only fall asleep if she is in the car. I know it is a bad habit, but we always have to drive her around the block to put her to sleep even when she wakes in the middle of the night. Thank goodness midnight drives only occur once or twice a week, but the situation nevertheless is now totally out of control. We are at our wits end. What should we do?

Sleep solution: If your baby has only ever associated sleep with the car, she will protest falling asleep in her cot in her sleep zone, so you need to take her through this transition slowly.

The first few days stop going out in the car at sleep times altogether. Stay in her sleep zone, and keep the movement consistent by pushing her in her pram, no matter how long it takes and how much she protests! When she is at the stage of falling asleep happily in the pram, then leave the pram still and let her fall asleep. Once she is falling asleep with no movement, put her straight into her cot at sleep time. Don't forget to always help her to get drowsy first. She may need some help in the form of patting and sitting with her for the first few days of being in her cot. Remain consistent, persevere and focus on your long-term goal, which is to teach your daughter to fall asleep independently. (Also read the advice on page 135.)

Quick relief for tired parents – toddler and preschooler

Have you noticed that everything in your life is now a negotiation? You need to be on top of the game to coax a wilful toddler to your way of thinking. Life is made up of constantly negotiating boundaries and picking your battles. Parenting a toddler is exhausting enough but add to that the fact that your last good night's sleep was when you were six months pregnant and you have a recipe for disaster.

WHAT TO EXPECT IN TERMS OF SLEEP AT THIS STAGE

- Your toddler should have all the strategies in place to be able to self-soothe and no longer needs any nutritional support at night.
- She should sleep for a stretch of 11 to 12 hours at night but occasional nights of disruption are normal through this stage. More than half of all toddlers wake up one night a week with a wet bed or a nightmare, but on the whole if she is comfortable, your child should be able to self-soothe back to sleep between sleep cycles.
- Bedtime should be between 6 & 7 pm, and your toddler will most likely wake for the day between 5 am and 7 am.
- During this stage your toddler may still need to sleep once a day for a period of one to three hours. The age at which your toddler drops her day sleep is very individual. One toddler will hold on to her day sleep until grade one, another will happily do without it from two and a half years old.
- Your older toddler may present with sleep problems based on the fact that she is at a stage of development when she is able to assert herself and push any boundaries you may have in place, particularly around bedtime.
- Undesirable sleep habits that may have begun in the first year of life are firmly entrenched by now.
- Owing to their growing imagination, toddlers do have more fears and frequently suffer from heightened separation anxiety, so sleep is naturally disrupted.
- Toddlers are also notoriously fussy eaters and nutritional needs may cause sleep issues.

GETTING IT RIGHT: THE BASICS

If you are still dealing with sleep issues or if they are a new development, you need to address the following basic issues, before putting some sleep strategies into place. This section will help you make sure your toddler is nutritionally sound, healthy and not suffering from separation anxiety.

Rule out illness

Your social toddler is exposed to new germs daily and ill health is often a factor in disrupted sleep at this stage. Read Chapter 5 carefully to be sure that your toddler is not ill.

Rule out other health issues

Two of the main health issues to rule out in the toddler years are iron deficiency (if you have a fussy eater) and worms (as your toddler explores the sandpit amongst other places). Read Chapter 5 carefully to exclude these and other common health issues.

Your older toddler's nutritional needs

Your toddler **should** be eating the same food as the rest of the family. Since toddlers are often too busy to eat anything you will want to know how her possibly limited diet affects sleep:

- As long as she is growing, **don't worry** if she is a picky or poor eater. Her growth rate slows down at this age, which does account for some loss of appetite and she will appear to thrive on very little other than fresh air!
- Toddlers are often too busy to eat so do try to offer her **frequent small meals.** She will eat if she is hungry.
- Don't be tempted to replace a meal with milk – this will fill her up and lessen her appetite even more.
- **Don't force her** to eat something you know she does not enjoy – it will cause untold stress. Give her what you know she **will** eat.
- If she is not thriving, it is a good idea to add a **protein supplement** to her bedtime milk. This will ensure that she is not hungry during the night and will help her gain weight. Ask your pharmacist or clinic nurse to recommend an age-appropriate protein supplement or specialized milk.
- Because of your toddler's erratic eating habits, it is a good idea to give her a good **multivitamin and iron supplement** to ensure healthy growth and development.
- If your child is **healthy and thriving**, but is a poor eater, do not worry – nutrition (or lack thereof!) is seldom a cause of night waking at this age.
- Do not give your toddler any food or drink that contains **caffeine**, especially close to bedtime.

GETTING IT RIGHT: SETTING THE STAGE

Before looking at bedtime and sleep itself you need to be sure your toddler is primed for good sleep habits.

The sleep zone

If your toddler is consistently climbing out of her cot, it is time to move her into a bed. This usually occurs at around two years of age. Invest in a side bar and position her bed against a wall or a chest of drawers.

- Keep your toddler's sleep zone as calming as possible by limiting the amount of clutter.
- Toddlers rely very heavily on consistency and thus a consistent calming sleep zone is a must.
- Use white noise such as a fan, humidifier or a white noise CD to settle her and help her sleep deeper.
- To limit early morning wakings and to encourage the day sleep for as long as possible, make sure the room is dark enough for sleep – use block out lining for your curtaining
- Use a night-light, so that your toddler is never left alone in the dark. Her imagination is rampant at this age, which might make her fearful of dark shadows.
- Make sure her room is entirely safe so that she cannot harm herself

The value of a sleep soother

A sleep soother such as a blanket or a soft toy is still a necessary sleep and calming tool for your toddler. At this stage, limit its use to sleep time or when she is miserable or insecure. Keep the sleep soother in her bed so that bedtime holds that attraction of her special sensory comfort.

Deal with separation issues

Your toddler may be very clingy at this age, and may express fear of separation at bedtime or come through to your room for reassurance during the night. Be sure to read Chapter 8 for a full discussion on dealing with separation anxiety if you feel this is the root of the sleep problems. Remember to always say goodbye cheerfully when you leave your toddler, and to greet her happily when you return, to avoid creating anxiety around separation.

Movement stimulation

Make sure your toddler gets all the movement input and heavy muscle activity her body craves during the day. This stimulus is important for the development of gross motor-skills and is the reason your toddler is so busy. In the late afternoon introduce some intense movement input – 5 minutes of rocking in hammock or a swing twice in late afternoon or even more if she enjoys the movement.

If your toddler is watching TV or involved primarily in quiet or sedentary activities, she is more likely to wake at night. TV before bedtime in particular is a hindrance to good sleep habits. Stop TV altogether if your toddler has sleep problems.

Help your toddler to sleep during the day

Your toddler seeks an enormous amount of interaction and stimulation at this stage. If she is not having a nap or at least a rest during the day and is over-socialized, you will have bedtime battles and restless nights.

Avoid sensory overload and over-tiredness

Toddlers do not have the capacity to read their body's signals that they have had enough, and sensory overload is the outcome

- Look out for her signals that will tell you that she is getting over-stimulated, such as becoming clingy and irritable, refusing to eat or co-operate and biting and pushing other children.
- Limit her *awake time* to five to six hours and try to encourage a midday sleep or at least a rest in a quiet space at this time.
- Try to limit each play date to one hour per year of your toddler's age. For example your two year old can cope with two hours of social interaction before a tantrum or melt down ensues.
- Before your toddler's nap and at bedtime help her to wind down by trying to do at least 10 minutes of calming sensory input.

Continue to encourage a day sleep routine

Many older toddlers begin to resist their day nap and a day routine becomes something of the past. If she is over-tired and over-stimulated it is probably because she still needs this sleep. Try to keep some semblance of a day routine.

- Your toddler should still be having one sleep a day, usually around midday. Remember to act on her signals, and to keep her *awake time* to about 5 hours.
- If your preschooler (from 3 years old) is resisting her day sleep, but is really struggling to make it through the afternoon, she will most likely have a day sleep on alternate days. Follow her lead and if the day sleep does not happen, make bedtime earlier for that day.
- On days that the day sleep is dropped, all preschoolers need quiet time in their sleep zone when they return home at lunchtime.
- Offer your toddler a hearty snack, such as an egg on toast or a sandwich and yogurt or lunch just before her sleep, so if she sleeps for a long period of time through lunchtime it does not matter.
- Do not wake your toddler from her midday sleep, unless it is after 3 pm

GETTING IT RIGHT AT BEDTIME

If you are experiencing bedtime battles, a **bedtime routine** is a great tool. If there is no pattern to her bedtime rituals your toddler will not begin to recognize the necessary sensory cues that prompt sleep. Follow a simple bedtime routine to ease her into sleep quicker:

- Have a consistent time for bed with a predictable routine leading up to bedtime. Between six and seven o'clock in the evening is an appropriate time for bed. Bear in mind that if the day sleep has fallen away, an early bedtime is important. Warn her 5 minutes before the routine starts

- Start the evening routine with a soothing warm bath followed by a calming massage, if she enjoys it. Keep bath time relatively quiet and calm.
- When you take her out of the bath, wrap her snugly in a warmed towel and take her into her sleep zone.
- After bath, keep stimulation to a minimum and avoid rough play. The arrival home of a working parent is a time of much excitement. You must come home **before** bath if you want to play with your child. If you arrive home **after** bath, interactions must be calming and nurturing rather than loud and boisterous.
- Rub a few drops of *Rescue Remedy* (available from your pharmacy) directly onto her wrist and temple pulse points and on the soles of her feet.
- Spend special quality time, engaging in 'floor time' activities such as reading or quietly doing a puzzle. Make sure you have boundaries in place regarding how many activities or books, before it's into bed
- Dim the lights, and let her drink some warm milk (if she wants to) while lying in your arms for a last cuddle. Tuck her sleep soother into her arms and sing a little lullaby.
- When she is calm and relaxed, give her a last kiss and a cuddle, then tuck her into her bed.
- Say good night and leave the room.

If she won't settle (both day and night sleeps)

If you have followed all the steps so far, but your toddler resists staying in her bed at sleep time (whether it is during the day or at bedtime in the evening), it is important to implement some toddler sleep coaching techniques in the form of behaviour modification. Different to babies, sleep training with toddlers rests on reason and cause and effect. Boundaries and consistency become your biggest allies.

Chapter 9 deals with sleep coaching in great depth. Please do not embark on sleep coaching your toddler unless you have read the toddler section on page 96.

You have put your toddler to bed and she immediately jumps out of bed or begins delaying tactics. Use these four steps to sleep coach your toddler:

1. Put your toddler back in bed and sit with her. If she continues to jump around, does not stay in bed, makes demands or there are any other toddler antics:
   - **Respond** to her request: 'I know you want … (a snack).'
   - **Empathise** so she feels understood: 'I would love to … (get you a snack).'
   - **Give a reason:** 'But I/you can't … (have a snack in your bed because of crumbs).'
   - **Give a boundary:** 'If you lie down and go to sleep, I will sit with you until you fall asleep.'
   - **Give a consequence:** 'If you get up again, I will have to leave.'
     Then sit on her bed until she falls asleep. You must stick to your end of the deal if she sticks to hers.

2. If she instantly jumps out of bed, leave the room and shut the door until she indicates to you that she is back in bed. Even a two-year-old will get this right if you are firm and consistent. Do this every time she wakes the first night.

3. The following nights when she begins her bedtime antics, follow the same strategy. Once she has the idea and is staying in bed, you can make an excuse to leave her room before she is asleep, such as: 'I need to turn the kettle on but I will be back now.' Leave the room and return promptly so that she trusts you. Then sit with her until she falls asleep.

4. Thereafter, each night make the time spent out of the room a little longer, for example: 'I must finish the salad for Dad's supper, but I will be back in 5 minutes.' And return. After a few more nights, you will re-enter the room to find your toddler asleep.

If your toddler voices a fear about 'the bogey man', a very useful trick is to buy a plastic spray bottle from the supermarket. Fill it with coloured water, and label it 'bogey man spray'. As part of her bedtime ritual, allow her to spray her bed and around her sleep zone with this solution. This empowering gesture will help her to feel in control of her fears. Reassure her that she can use it again should she wake in the night.

SLEEP SECRET

- Only sleep train if you are certain that all the basics have been ruled out as causes for night wakings and only if you and your partner agree on the strategies.
- Some habits are hard to break, and if your toddler has been crying a lot, she may need to sip on some cooled boiled water to quench her thirst. Add a few drops of Rescue Remedy to her water. (One drop per kilogram of your toddler's weight)
- If your toddler is ill, all rules go out the window. This is a time to love and nurture her until she is well. If any bad habits become entrenched, simply deal with them when she is well again.
- Be sure to meet your toddler's needs during the day and to give her lots of love and cuddles.

Bedtime boundary issues

Boundaries need to be set clearly, and negotiations can happen within these predetermined boundaries. Your toddler needs to understand clearly the sleep boundaries you have for her. All the role players in the care of your toddler need to agree on sleep boundaries. **Right now** think through and create and agree on boundaries on the following issues:

- Where is your toddler's sleep zone?
- What time is bedtime?
- How long will a parent sit with her?

- How many books can be read before lights out?
- No drinks or food in her bed?
- If she wakes in the night what is the procedure?
- If she has a nightmare, where can she sleep?

Once you have predetermined these boundaries, you need to have consistent associated consequences, so let your behaviour do the talking when it comes to sleep – try to avoid the trap of continually negotiating, explaining or threatening.

*Teach your toddler these sleep rules early and repeat them often:

At bedtime we
stay in bed
close our eyes
stay very quiet and
*go to sleep.**

*(adapted from *Toddler sense.* Ann Richardson. Metz Press. 2005)

GETTING IT RIGHT AT NIGHT

Many toddlers wake at night. To foster independence and self-soothing without intervention from you, it is essential your toddler has a sleep soother or blanky which she can use successfully when she wakes at night.

Toddler coming through at night

At some stage during this period, many toddlers wake up and wander through to their parent's bedroom. Begin by instilling a boundary and consistently lead your toddler back to her bed when this happens. The goal is to have your toddler sleep in **her bed**.

Once your toddler is generally sleeping in her bed, you may still find she has the odd night when she is very distressed when she wakes. These are the times when she may be distraught owing to a nightmare and imagination fears or separation anxiety (common in the toddler years). When this happens you may need to allow her to sleep **next to your bed**. By not allowing her into your bed and not making her makeshift bed *too* comfortable, you will not instil long-lasting habits.

Know that it will not last forever and is usually a passing stage. If it becomes a nightly occurrence and is a problem for you, start to make it less easy for her to do. **Always** take her back to her room first. If she insists on returning to your bedroom let her carry her own bedding and settle herself.

Toddler in your bed

If your toddler is persistently coming through to you at night, and insisting on getting into **your bed**, this again is a scenario that you could leave as it is if it is not an issue with you. If you would like to reclaim your sleep space, allow her to sleep on a mattress or some continental pillows next to your bed to help her with the transition to **her own room**.

- Remember always to acknowledge her feelings: 'I know you want to be in the bed with me.'
- Then mirror the feeling by saying: 'I love having you in the bed.'"
- Then give a reason why she can't be in the bed with you: 'This is my bed, and there is too little space now that you are bigger.'
- Offer an alternative: "Why don't you lie on the floor next to me and I'll hold your hand." You will need to follow through on this boundary and be firm about her not getting back into your bed. If she will not lie on the floor next to you, take her back to her bed. At this point, you may have to start adopting some sleep coaching strategies (see page 87).

Allowing your toddler to sleep on the floor next to you while you are undoing the undesirable sleep habit of having her in your bed, is a necessary process you will need to undertake while you foster confidence in her to become independent.

> SLEEP SECRET
> *Allowing your toddler to sleep next to your bed is a step in the direction of sleep independence.*

Night feeds

Many toddlers may wake at night demanding a bottle of milk or juice. To wean her off this habit, take your toddler on an outing to buy her special night-time cup/sippy cup. As part of the bedtime ritual allow her to fill it with **water** and place it next to her bed. Tell her before she goes to sleep that there will be no bottles during the night and that if she is thirsty, she has her water to sip on. When she wakes in the middle of the night insisting on a hot drink, simply give the boundary: 'No, we don't have bottles at night; here is your sleep blanky. If you are thirsty your special water is next to your bed; now go to sleep.' Here no negotiation is needed.

COMMON SLEEP ISSUES IN TODDLERS AND PRESCHOOLERS
Toddler separation anxiety

My two-year-old has suddenly become very anxious, especially at bedtime and when I have to leave the house. I have recently started a mornings-only job – could this be the reason. She eats well and seems happy and content in all other ways. How do I get her to be less clingy?

Sleep solution: Two-year-olds are still very emotionally needy, so she may well be having some separation issues about you leaving the house. This may also be the reason why she is worried about separating from you at bedtime. Talk to her about separating from her to go to work or to the shops as part of your normal conversation. Make up stories about other moms who work and have to go away from home for a short while, but who always come back, and who will always love their children. There are some lovely books and CDs/tapes available that deal with the issue of separation in story form which are most beneficial (see Useful Resources, page 168). Always remain upbeat about leaving the house or separating from her at bedtime, so that she does not pick up any anxiety about the separation on your part.

Distraction is the best bet when the actual separation is imminent. Try to instil a ritual around leaving the house such as 'helping mom find her car keys', always followed by a special treat such as a push on her swing, or a special song, with her and her care-giver when you leave. Pop a few pictures of yourself and the family into a mini photograph album, so that she can see you when you are not there, or let her drape a special scarf of yours around her neck, and ask her to 'look after it for mommy'. Use these strategies at bedtime too. Take her on a special outing to purchase a 'special night-time friend' such as a soft toy, for her to take to bed with her at night. Make the effort to spend some time alone with her without any distractions during the day, and before bed, which will help her to feel secure. Separation anxiety is a completely normal part of development, so don't worry unduly.

Dummy to sleep

My two-and-a-half-year-old still has a dummy when she sleeps. Is this a bad thing to still be attached to at this age? My mother is putting pressure on me to get rid of it, but it really helps her to sleep well.

Sleep solution: There is a reason why dummies are called pacifiers! As long as your daughter is using her dummy to pacify herself in an appropriate manner such as when she is tired and crabby, or in a strange and menacing environment such as a doctor's visit, don't worry about it for now. However, if she is unduly attached to her dummy, and seems to need it all the time, then I would suggest some gentle persuasion to use it only for really needy occasions. Having a dummy in her mouth all the time will hamper her speech development and may cause possible teeth deformities. When she demands her dummy to suck upon, and it is not sleep time, and she is in an un-threatening environment, distraction usually works well. Have a bag of tricks handy, such as little trinkets, stickers, or even a little sweet. Offer her one treat in place of her dummy and praise and encourage her for doing without the dummy at that moment. Always acknowledge her need for the dummy, by saying: 'I know you want your dummy right now, and I'd like to give it to you, but we don't have it with us now, so how about choosing a sticker instead?' Expect her to complain, but remain firm and calm, and she will soon be distracted by the trinket.

She will get rid of her dummy at sleep time when she is ready. It is always helpful to encourage her to try other ways of calming, such as a soft toy, or special blanket. Another useful way to get rid of the dummy is to get the Easter Bunny or The Dustbin Man to take it away. Offer her a coveted item as a replacement, and once the deal is negotiated and agreed on, don't go back on what you have decided — this will only confuse her!

> **SLEEP SECRET**
> Being in tune with your toddler's sensory system and watching and understanding her signals to you are the first steps towards better sleep. Structure and routine, early to bed and teaching her healthy sleep habits will really help calm down a busy or 'hyperactive' child.

Moving to a bed

My two-year-old can now climb out of her cot. She has always gone to sleep happily on her own, but now runs out of her room and thinks it is playtime. My husband and I do not want to have to stay with her in her room until all hours of the night. We have tried closing the door but she cries until she sometimes vomits. How on earth do we continue with sleep training?

Sleep solution: It sounds like she has outgrown her cot, and needs to make the transition into a big bed. Invest in a side bar, and position her bed against a wall or chest of drawers. Make sure she is well and healthy and emotionally secure. Let her choose a special pillowcase or soft toy, and re-enforce the idea that her bed is a lovely place to sleep, and then follow these simple guidelines. Remember you are the adult in this situation, and it is up to you to remain the one in charge.

- Have bedtime rituals that involve time spent cuddling, story time, then a firm and loving 'goodnight'.
- Leave a night light on in her room so that she is never alone in the dark.
- Offer her the option of keeping the door open if she will stay in her bed.
- If she does not want to stay in her bed, tell her that you will have to close the door. Negotiate this with her once or twice. If you have to close the door, do not slam it shut.
- She will get out of bed and cry and bang on the door. Wait for a minute or two, then go back and comfort her and stay with her till she is calm. Resist the temptation to shout and admonish. Reassure her that she is safe and that you love her, but that it is now bedtime and the rule is that she must stay in bed, otherwise you will have to close the door.
- When she is calm again (this may take some time, so be prepared), negotiate with her about whether the door stays open or closed, re-enforcing the rule that the door can stay open as long as she stays in her bed. If she keeps coming out, then close the door once more. This time, wait for an extra few minutes until you go back in to her room to comfort and calm her.
- Always praise her if she stays in her bed
- Continue with this routine until she eventually falls asleep.

It is unlikely she will cry long enough to vomit with this method. If she does vomit after a short period of crying, she may be doing so as a manipulative ploy to get her own way, so do keep calm, focused and in control. She needs to know this in order to respond to your wishes.

SENSORY PROCESSING PROBLEMS AND SLEEP

At 6 months old, Jadyn was the most difficult baby imaginable. He was hypersensitive to touch, smells and movement and tolerated almost no nurturing cuddles. He continued to have colic, way beyond the age that colic disappears and he had never slept longer than 20 minutes, day or night. Not surprisingly, his mother was suffering from postnatal depression and all relationships within the home were under terrible strain.

Most babies fall within the normal range of sleep problems which are relatively simple to correct, with just a few changes to sensory environment, routine, diet and some behavioural management. If your baby responded well to the strategies outlined in this book, you can rest assured that you are not dealing with deep-seated sensory issues. However, if you have tried everything and have a baby who is not only a poor sleeper, but also exhibits other areas of difficulty, such as feeding issues and behaviour problems, you could well be looking at a sensory processing problem as a basis for a long term complicated sleep disorder.

SENSORY PROCESSING PROBLEMS

Sensory processing problems may be the cause of sleep problems if
- Your baby was very colicky and fussy for more than four months
- Your baby or toddler is over sensitive to touch, sounds and smells, reacting by withdrawing or crying to any of these stimuli
- Your toddler is excessively busy, seeking movement and falling a lot
- Your baby or toddler is excessively restless at night
- Your baby head bangs for hours in the middle of the night
- Your baby or toddler suffers repeated night terrors.

THREE GROUPS OF SENSORY PROCESSING PROBLEMS IMPACT ON SLEEP

If you are concerned about sensory processing difficulties in your baby you will want to seek out professional help, however the following summaries of how sensory processing difficulties affect sleep may help you understand why your baby's sleep problem has developed.

Sensory defensiveness
For the majority of people, the normal sensory experiences of life are pleasurable most of the time. But for sensory defensive children, random sensory input is perceived as painful and irritating. They are more sensitive to either some or all modes of input.

This sensory sensitivity results in sleep problems for the following reasons:

Auditory defensiveness results in waking due to being roused by sounds that would not wake most babies, such as a door opening or a phone ringing a few rooms away. These babies rarely fall into deep sleep states as their sensitivity to sounds keeps them conscious of noise.

To help your baby sleep deeper, use white noise in the room as white noise absorbs irregular sounds and will help your baby ignore sounds that otherwise would wake him. The best sources of white noise are:

- *Running water*
- *Vacuum cleaner*
- *White noise CD's*
- *Fan*
- *Humidifier*

Tactile defensive babies are woken by touch irritants such as a label or seam in their clothing or rough sheets that would not affect other babies. Light touch just before bedtime also makes them irritable and less likely to fall asleep.

Hold your baby firmly just before bed and during feeds as light intermittent touch is alerting. Use clothes without labels or cut them out, use very soft sheets and blankets.

Olfactory defensiveness is sensitivity to smells and often associated tastes too. These babies' sleep may be disturbed by a subtle detergent odour we are not even aware of.

Try not to use any fragranced products when washing your baby's clothes or even on your baby's skin if they are olfactory defensive.

If your baby has sensory defensiveness and is not sleeping well you have a cycle that develops: the more sleep deprived a child is, the more sensory defensive he becomes and in turn the worse he sleeps. It really is vital that this cycle is broken.

Vestibular-proprioceptive processing problems

Knowing how important movement and deep pressure are for sleep (Chapter 2) it stands to reason that babies who do not process movement well may have sleep problems:

Movement sensitivity causes babies and toddlers find movement threatening and so they avoid movement. These babies do not enjoy being thrown in the air or dipped backwards. They are happier to be sitting still and may have delayed motor milestones, such as rolling and crawling. The lack of movement input during the day can result in wakings at night.

Even though your baby is sensitive to movement he does need the input in order to sleep well. By using comforting movement, such as being carried or going for a ride in the pram you can make sure your baby receives movement stimuli. Gradually increase the amount of movement your baby tolerates by introducing new movement experiences each day. Always act within your baby's enjoyment levels.

Proprioceptive defensiveness is rare but results in resistance to bear weight on the legs and even the arms. These babies do not like to crawl or roll and often miss these milestones completely. When you hold your baby under the arms in a standing position, he will pull his legs up and try not to carry any weight on his legs. The regulating and calming effect of deep pressure is not accessed by these children and aside from being more fussy, they do not sleep well. They are also the children who dislike being covered with blankets at all.

Deep pressure massage and swaddling are vital for these babies. Try different weights of duvet to ascertain what covering your toddler will best tolerate.

Movement seeking is seen in very busy babies. These children do not sense movement optimally and seek faster, rougher and more movement than most. At nights they wake to jump in their cots or head bang or rock.

Adding in more controlled movement in combination with deep pressure, such as tug of war or rough and tumble with dad or hanging on a bar swing that is just above their reach, will help these babies.

High arousal levels

Imagine that you are trying to fall asleep, when suddenly you hear a strange sound in the house and then your house alarm goes off. You go and check what the sound was and discover it was only the wind. Chances are that you will battle to fall back to sleep quickly. When you are anxious or in an environment that threatens you, your arousal levels are heightened, resulting in a flight, fright or fight response. Babies with sensory defensiveness are threatened by normal, innoxious sensory information, resulting in adrenaline being released. They really do find it very hard therefore to drop off to sleep and are easily wakened.

SOLUTIONS FOR SLEEP PROBLEMS RELATED TO SENSORY PROCESSING PROBLEMS

There is no simple solution for these babies and intervention from an occupational therapist specialized in sensory integration is needed. The intervention will work both on improving sensory processing, as well as strategies to help your baby cope with the sensory information he has difficulty processing.

To minimise the effects of sensory issues on sleep:

- A baby who is over-sensitive to sensory input is much more susceptible to over-stimulation than most so be aware of his signals of over-stimulation (see page 61). When your baby shows signs of over-stimulation, remove him from the environment and retreat to quiet space or the outdoors to settle him.
- Your baby's lower threshold for sensory information means that social situations need to be predictable and short. Make sure your baby does socialise but make the groups small and choose playmates that are quieter and less likely

to overwhelm your baby. You may need to shorten the time spent socialising until your baby is coping better with all the input.

- Use sensory calming strategies consistently before bedtime. Calming sensory input includes: soothing massage, rocking, lavender oil in a burner (out of reach) in his room, deep pressure in the form of a weighted blanket if your baby is over 12 months.
- Routine and predictability are critical with these babies. Their world is so unpredictable on a sensory level and they do very well with rigid routines and predictable events. Keep their sleep environment and bedtime routine consistent, even when you have to go on holiday or away.
- Do not co-sleep with your baby. Sensitive babies sleep worse in their parent's beds and yet they are often the ones where parents revert to co-sleeping, as they are too exhausted to get up repeatedly at night. In your bed, your baby is subjected to lots of extra sensory information that stimulates him at night; sheets moving when you turn over, light touch as your body brushes him and dad's snores and splutters.
- Work through steps 1 to 8 of this book, but do not sleep train your baby or do any form of sleep behaviour modification until you have dealt with the sensory issues in therapy with a therapist. Sleep coaching generally does not work and can even exacerbate these sleep problems.

If you are dealing with a fussy baby or busy toddler and on top of that he has very poor sleep habits, you will feel desperate at times. These are a few practical tips to help you:

- Understanding why your baby is as he is will help you in normalising your situation as well as seeking the right advice as you embark on the process of helping your baby.
- Get support in the form of counselling or a support group as you will be in need of validation and support to keep yourself strong to help your baby overcome his difficulties.
- Do not be tempted to compare your self or your baby to others, as you will end up feeling inadequate as a mother. This condition is real and you are not to blame.

SPECIFIC SLEEP PROBLEMS

Mary wakes every night screaming out loud. Her mother panics and jumps out of bed each night, thinking something terrible is happening to Mary. And each night it's the same thing, just a nightmare. The truth is though, for Mary this is something terrible and her mom needs to broach the problem sensitively.

NIGHTMARES

Before a year of age your baby does not have language with which to label the visual images in her mind. For this reason imagination is thought to only really develop after eighteen months, when language is exploding. At this age, your toddler's imagination can become overwhelming, as the concept of fears and boogey men arise. Your toddler may start exhibiting nightmares, which are a normal part of her development. Nightmares are part of normal sleep, occur during the light sleep phase, and are not necessarily associated with any specific emotional problem. Because your toddler is in light sleep when the nightmare occurs, she will wake easily and be able to remember what happened in her dream. You will be able to easily console her and re-settle her back to sleep when she is feeling better.

Coping with nightmares

- Respond with love and cuddles when she has a nightmare.
- Keep a night-light on in her room, or leave a bathroom or passage light on at night.
- After your toddler has experienced a nightmare, she may be frightened and not want to separate from you. Keep a small mattress or some continental pillows next to your bed, so if she comes through to you after waking from a nightmare, she can sleep next to you for the rest of the night.
- Stop all TV viewing as at this age your child cannot separate TV from reality
- Deal with fears of separation verbally during the day.

NIGHT TERRORS

Night terrors are different from nightmares as your child does not always wake up but screams in a terror. She may well show physical signs of physical distress such as sweating, rapid heart rate or bulging eyes. The worst part is that she may not respond to you, or be aware of anything else in the environment. This can be very disturbing to you, as a night terror may last a long time, and your child may even strike out at you when you seek to comfort her. Different from nightmares, night terrors can be seen in young babies (although the most common age of occurrence is between two and five years old) as they are not due to imagination and therefore not dependant on language development. Night terrors are not bad dreams, and actually occur when she is sleeping deeply. They usually occur within the first part of the night, within 1-3 hours after she has fallen asleep. At the end of her deep sleep cycle (as she enters REM sleep), one part of her brain wakes up, but another stays in a deep sleep state (this is due to an immaturity of her nervous system). This results in a 'night terror' when she is seemingly awake, but is actually in a deep sleep. The brain is likely to associate fear with the physical symptoms of the night terror such as rapid heart rate and sweating, and this is why your child may cry and scream during an episode. In some cases high fevers can cause night terrors owing to disruptions in the sleep cycle. Night terrors are seldom caused by psychological trauma, and most children return to sleep easily once it is over, and have no recollection of the episode the next day.

Coping with night terrors

- There is not much you can do for your child when she is having a night terror, other than holding her tightly and reassuring her that you are there. Sometimes touching her may cause unnecessary stimulation, making it worse, so you may have to simply wait it out while keeping her safe.
- Research has shown that night terrors are common in children with abnormal sleep schedules and fatigue. By sticking to the awake times and implementing a regular day sleep and bedtime routine you can avert night terrors.
- If your child is experiencing night terrors, try to encourage a daytime nap, move her bedtime earlier and avoid excessive stimulation and sensory overload during the day, particularly before bedtime.
- If your child is experiencing frequent night terrors, it is sometimes useful to try waking her 15 minutes before you know it is going to occur (you will have to ascertain this time by keeping a sleep diary for a few nights). Keep her fully awake for about 5-10 minutes, then re-settle her for the night. Do this for seven to eight consecutive nights, then stop waking her. The 'fault' in her deep sleep phase should have corrected itself by then.

HEAD BANGING AND BODY ROCKING

About 5-10 per cent of children, usually boys, will bang or roll their heads before falling asleep. In most children this is a normal part of development and should stop by the time they are four years old. This rhythmic behaviour is often due to a sensory need such as the need for movement or proprioception. Some babies use the movement to self regulate when feeling over-stimulated and over-tired. By moving their bodies rhythmically, the arousal system is regulated, and the children feel calmer and more grounded.

Coping with head banging and body rocking

- Avoid over-tiredness and over-stimulation by encouraging a day nap or some regular quiet time, and move bedtime earlier.

• Try to encourage your toddler to participate in more intensive movement and heavy work during the day (pushing or pulling a loaded barrow and lots of outdoor play).

• Very rarely, head banging and body rocking are associated with underlying neurological diseases. Your paediatrician will be able to diagnose these uncommon conditions if they are present, so if you are worried, please seek medical help.

TWINS/MULTIPLES AND SLEEP

Jenny had so badly wished for her own babies. Five years down the line of fertility treatment and three IVFs later, Jenny got her wish - threefold! Triplets were the most work she had ever had. The hardest part was that none of the three was sleeping well because they kept setting each other off. Jenny was exhausted and at a loss as to how to sleep-train her busy 10-month-olds.

Because of infertility treatment these days, it is a well-known phenomenon that we are seeing more and more multiple (mainly twin) births. When you bring your babies home, there will undoubtedly be much work involved, especially in the early days. A strong structure and routine will play an important role in helping you stay sane and reasonably rested in these hectic first weeks.

THE IMPORTANCE OF ROUTINE

The demands of parenting these helpless little bundles will mean that for now, decent sleep is a long distant memory. With multiple babies, routine is the key to keeping a structure in place that will ultimately help you to get more sleep.

- Get help, whether that means recruiting a family member or hiring a nanny. This is important, especially if you have a toddler as well.
- One baby may be more demanding than the other, which may throw you a bit, but once you know how to handle each baby, respond to their individual signals and work around that, life will start settling into a routine of sorts. It is advisable to set feeding times strongly. Demand feeding multiples is very difficult as the chance of rest anywhere along the line is slim. It is possible to breastfeed multiples. Some moms like to feed simultaneously with one baby feeding on each breast, while some prefer to feed them straight after each other, a few minutes apart.
- Another idea to allow you to have some more rest is to alternate their feeds; breast milk for one feed and formula for the next feed.
- Remember your babies are individuals, and may have digestive systems that function differently, so if they are being bottle fed it is possible that they may need to be on different formulas! The same applies to solid food and meal planning.
- Their nervous systems may also function differently. Your babies' sleep needs may differ with one needing more sleep than the other. One of your babies may cope better with prolonged stimulation than her sister or brother. Remember consider each baby as an individual
- In the early days, let your babies sleep together. They were together in the womb and being together can be comforting
- Try to get them synchronised into the same routines of sleep, wake and play

(even if the meals and activities may be slightly different), so that their body clocks and biorhythms are as similar as possible, but if they are very different, accept that they may be 'out of synch' for some periods of time.
• Separate them from sleeping together if one is sick, if they keep very different awake and play times, or if you are trying to sleep-train one of them.
• Keep a log of all feeds and sleeps, as it is really easy to get confused about which baby has done what

SLEEP COACHING

Should you have to address undesirable sleep habits in any one of your babies (or all of them), you must treat them as individuals. It is impossible to sleep-train multiples at once. Separate them so that they don't disturb one another. Enlist some support in the form of a night nurse or a family member who can take care of the other baby(ies) while you are sleep training.

You may become a little socially unacceptable after the birth of your multiples. A mother of multiples becomes an entourage, and if you have toddlers even more so. Don't fret! Find similar moms through an organization such as SAMBA (South African Multiple Birth Association on 0861 432 432 or www.samultiplebirth.co.za) with whom to swap war stories, learn what to expect and engage in twin or triplet-friendly activities.

USEFUL RESOURCES

BOOKS FOR KIDS

Separation anxiety

The good-bye book by Judith Viorst. Schuster Children's Publishing Division. New York 1988

The kissing hand by Audrey Penn. Tanglewood Press Inc. USA. May 2006

Even if I spill my milk by Anita Grossnickle Hines. Houghton-mifflin. 1994

Benjamin comes back by Amy Brandt. Childcare Books for Kids. 1999

Sleep time

Good night Moon by Margaret Wise Brown. Harper Collins Publishers, Mexico. 1991

My goodnight book. A Golden Book Western Publishing Company Inc. New York. 1981

Time for Bed P.B. Bear A Dorling Kindersley Book. London. 1998

All About Bedtime Time Life Books, Amsterdam. 1989

Can't you sleep little bear? by Martin Waddell. Candlewick Press, Hong Kong. 1994

It's bedtime Wibbly Pig by Mick Inkpen. Hodder Children's Books, USA. 2004

Guess how much I love you by Sam McBratney. Candlewick Press,USA. 1995

BOOKS FOR PARENTS

Breastfeeding books

Dr Miriam Stoppard Complete Baby and Childcare. D.K. Publishing. London. 2006

Breastfeeding: The Essential Guide by Sharon Trotter. 2004

Breastfeeding for beginners by Caroline Deacon. National Childbirth Trust. 2002

Breastfeeding: A practical guide for parents by Johnsons. DK Publishers. 2006

Recipe and diet book

Annabel Karmel's New complete baby and toddler meal planner. Random House. 2004.

Lorraine Kelly's Baby and Toddler Eating Plan: Over 100 Healthy, Quick and Easy Recipes by Lorraine Kelly and Anita Bean. Virgin books 2004.

Baby & Child Care books

Baby Sense: Megan Faure, Ann Richardson: Metz Press 2002

Toddler Sense: Ann Richardson: Metz Press 2005

LULLABIES

Golden slumbers

Golden slumbers kiss your eyes,
Smiles await you when you rise.
Sleep pretty baby,
Do not cry,
And I will sing a lullaby.
Thomas Dekker (16th-17th Century)

Sleep, baby, sleep

Sleep, baby, sleep,
Your father tends the sheep
Your mother shakes
The dreamland tree,
And from it falls sweet
Dreams for thee.
Sleep, baby, sleep,
Sleep, baby, sleep.
Unknown

Hush little baby

Hush little baby, don't say a word,
Papa's gonna buy you a mockingbird
And if that mockingbird won't sing,
Papa's gonna buy you a diamond ring.
And if that diamond ring turns brass,
Papa's gonna buy you a looking glass.
And if that looking glass falls down,
You'll still be the sweetest baby in town.
Unknown

Rock a bye baby

Rock-a-bye baby, in the tree top
When the wind blows, the cradle will rock
When the bough breaks, the cradle will fall
And down will come baby, cradle and all
Unknown (1600's)

Lullaby and good night

Lullaby and good night,
With roses bedight,
With lilies o'er spread,
Is baby's wee bed,
Lay you down now, and rest,
May your slumber be blessed!
Lay you down now, and rest,
May your slumber be blessed!
Johannes Brahms (1868)

I see the moon

I see the moon,
And the moon sees me.
God Bless the moon,
God Bless me!
(Anonymous)

Twinkle, twinkle, little star

Twinkle, twinkle, little star,
How I wonder what you are!
Up above the world so high
Like a diamond in the sky.
Twinkle, twinkle, little star,
How I wonder what you are!
Jane Taylor,
(All About Bedtime: Time Life books 1989)

My bed is warm and cosy

My bed is warm and cosy.
My mum's turned off the light.
I think I'll close my eyes... and ears...
And go to sleep. Good night!
Adapted from 'Sounds at night' Joan Israel
(All About Bedtime: Time Life books 1989)

Thula baba

Thula thul' thula baba thula sana
Thula mam uzo buya eku seni
Thula thul' thula baba thula sana
Thula mam uzo buya eku seni

Kukwi nkanyesi
ekanyel umama
imkanyi sela
indlele zyeh kaya

Thula thula thula baba
Thula thula thula sana
Thula thula thula baba
Thula thula thula san
Traditional Xhosa lullabye

WEBSITES

www.toddlersense.co.za
www.babysense.com
www.sleepfoundation.org
www.babycentre.co.uk
www.mumsnet.co.uk
www.babysleepshop.com
www.nct.org.uk
www.tipslimited.com
www.midwivesonline.com

CD'S FOR SLEEP

Baby Sense™ Womb to World CD –
Soothing womb sounds and white noise to lull, calm and induce sleep.
Rocking Chair Meditation Music –
Meditation music for pregnant women and new parents.
Digifest 2006. www.babynature.co.za

REFERENCES

Allen, LH: *Proposed fortification levels for Complementary foods for Young children.* Journal Nutrition, 2003

Anders, T; Halpern, L and Hua, J: *Sleeping through the night: A developmental perspective.* Pediatrics Vol 90 No 4, October 1992

Barral, Joelle: *When dreams mix up with reality.* http://www.stanford.edu/~jbarral/Downloads/Neuro-Rapport.pdf

Bly, L: *Motor Skills Acquisition Checklist* Therapy Skill Builders, 2000

Cambell, G. & Devins, M: *The World's Most Amazing Science Facts for Kids.* Egmont Books Limited, 2005

Corken, G: *Worm Infestations.* Pharmacy management, September 1993

Davis, KF; Parker, KP & Montgomery, GL: *Sleep in Infants and Young Children: Part One: Normal Sleep.* Journal of Pediatric Health Care 18(2), 2004

Daws, D: *Sleep problems in babies and young children.* Journal of Child Psychotherapy, 11(2), 1985

De Gangi, G: *Pediatric Disorders of Regulation in Affect and Behaviour.* Academic Press, 2000

Derman, DP; Bothwell, TH and MacPhail, SP et al: *Importance of Ascorbic Acid in the absorption of iron from infant foods.* Scan Journal of Haematology, 1980

Eberlein, T: *Sleep: how to teach your child to sleep like a baby.* Pocket Books, N Y, 1996

Eliot, L *What's going on in there? How the brain and mind develop in the first five years of life.* Penguin Books Limited, 2000

Faber, M: et al: *The effect of a low cost micro-nutrient fortified cereal on the nutritional status of infants.* MRC report, February 2004

Faure, M & Richardson, A: *Baby Sense.* Metz Press, South Africa, 2002

Ferber, R: *Solve your child's sleep problems.* Dorling Kindersley, London 1985

Geldenhuys, Dr C: *Sleep Smart.* Rollerbird Press, South Africa, 2003

Gerard, CM; Harris, KA & Thach, BT: *Spontaneous Arousals in Supine Infants While Swaddled and Unswaddled During Rapid Eye Movement and Quiet Sleep.* Pediatrics Vol 110, No 6, 2002

Gerhardt, S: *Why love matters – How affection shapes a baby's brain.* Brunner Routledge, 2004

Gorman, C: *Why we sleep.* TIME magazine, January 24, 2005

Haus, E: *The development of the human time structure from childhood to senescence.* The American Association of Medical Chronobiology and Chronotherapuetics, 2004

Hiscockm H & Wakem M: *Infant Sleep Problems and Postnatal Depression: A community-Based Study.* Pediatrics Vol 107, No 6, June 2001

Holford, Dr Patrick: *The Optimum Nutrition Bible.* Piatkus London, 1997

Holly, A DiLeo: *Chronobiology, melatonin, and sleep in infants and children.* Pediatric Nursing, January 2002

Hughes, David B and Hoover, Dallas G: *Bifidobacteria: Their Potential for Use in American Dairy Products.* Food Technology, April, 1991

Hui-Chin: *Hsu Antecedents and consequences of separation anxiety in first-time mothers: infant, mother and social-contextual characteristics.* Infant Behaviour & Development Vol 27, Issue 2, May 2004

Huntley, R: *The Sleep Book for Tired Parents.* Souvenir Press, London, 1997

Isolauri, E & Arvola, T et al: *Probiotics in the management of atopic eczema.* Clinical and Experimaental Allergy, Vol 30, 2000

Jenni, OG & Carskadon, MA: *Normal Human Sleep at Different Ages: Infants to Adolescents* In: *Sleep Research Society. SRS Basics of Sleep Guide,* Sleep Research Society, Westchester, Illinois, 2005

Johnson & Johnson Pediatric Institute: *Emotional Regulation and Developmental Health in Infancy and Early Childhood,* LLC, 2002

Johnson, CM: *Helping Infants Learn To Sleep.* Paediatric Basics, 2000

Lulter, CK & Dewey, KGI: *Proposed Nutrient Composition for Fortified Complementary Foods.* Journal of Nutrition, 2003

Lutz, WJ & Hock, E: *Maternal separation anxiety: relations to adult attachment representations in mothers of infants.* Journal of Genetic Psychology, March 1995 156(1)

Majamaa, H & Isolauri, E: *Probiotics: A novel approach in the management of food allergy.* Journal Allergy Clinical Immunology February, 1997

Mitsuoka, T: *Intestinal Bacteria and Health,* 1978

Paediatric Hotline: Vol 2, Issue 3, 1993

Piccini, C: *Training Manual for Infant Nutrition:* Nutricia, 2002

Richardson, A: *Toddler Sense.* Metz Press, South Africa, 2005

Ross, CN & Karraker, KH: *Effects of Fatigue on Infant Emotional Reactivity and Regulation.* Infant mental health Journal, Vol 20 (4) 1999

Russo, MB: *Normal Sleep, Sleep Physiology, and Sleep Deprivation: General Principles* http://www.emedicine.com/neuro/topic444.htm 2005

Scher, A; Hershkovitz, R; & Harel, J: *Maternal separation anxiety in infancy: precursors and outcomes.* Child Psychiatry Human Development, 1998 29(2)

Scher, A & Blumberg, O: *Night waking among 1-year olds: a study of maternal separation anxiety.* Child: Care, Health and Development Vol 25, No 5, September 1999

Schmidt, Wolfgang A: *Toll of allergy reduced by probiotics.* M Kalliomaki, S Salminen et.al *Probiotics in primary prevention of atopic disease.* The Lancet. Vol 357, April 2001

Shaw, R: *The Epidemic.* Harper Collins, 2003

Sunderland, M: *The Science of Parenting.* Dorling Kindersley, 2006

Van Niekerk, M: *Monster Busting.* Unisa Press. Pretoria, 1998

Van Uytvanghe, Dr C: *Additional Feeding, Supplementary Vitamins and Allergic Conditions.* South Africa, 1994

Weissbluth, Dr M: *Healthy Sleep Habits, Happy Child.* Ballantine Book, NY, 1999

Weissbluth, Dr M: *Your Fussy Baby.* Ballantine Books, NY, 2003

Zilibowitz, M: *A Watch, Wait and Wonder Parent – Child Interaction Programme.* Lecture at Western Cape Association of Infant Mental Health, February 2006

Zuckerman, Dr M: *Gastro Oesophageal Reflux.* CBERG, March 2006

Baby Sense™

calming and sleep products for babies

visit www.babysense.com to view the ever-expanding product range

calm

All Baby Sense™ products have been designed by Megan Faure (occupational therapist) and co-author of *Sleep sense* and *Baby sense*.

Baby sense (book)
Best selling baby care book, addressing the most common concerns parents have during their baby's first year, from a sensory perspective.

Sling
The Baby Sense™ Sling encourages moms and dads to "wear" their babies in the optimal position.

Toddler sense (book)
Knowing what constitutes normal toddler behaviour leads to effective, guilt-free and realistic parenting.

Cuddlewrap
The Baby Sense™ Cuddlewrap is the the perfect wrap for a new baby.

sleep

Slumber Sac
The Baby Sense™ Slumber Sac is made from 100% cotton for warmth.

Sleep sense (book)
Simple steps to a good night sleep based on sensory integration principles.

Taglet
The Baby Sense™ Taglet is the ultimate 'sleep blanky'.

Womb to World cd
White noise to help baby sleep and limit crying.

www.babysense.com